MYTHOLOGICAL CREATURES

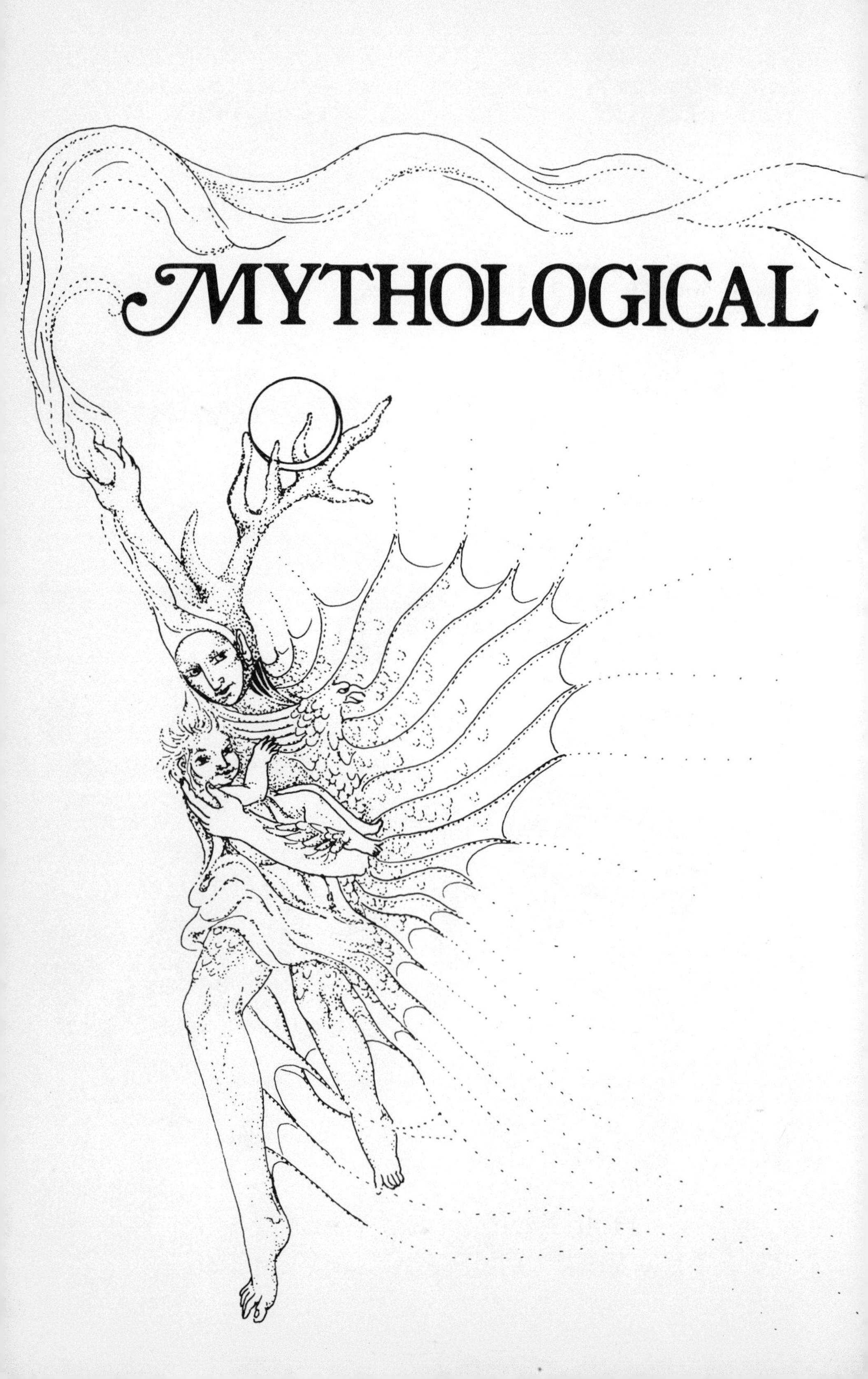
MYTHOLOGICAL

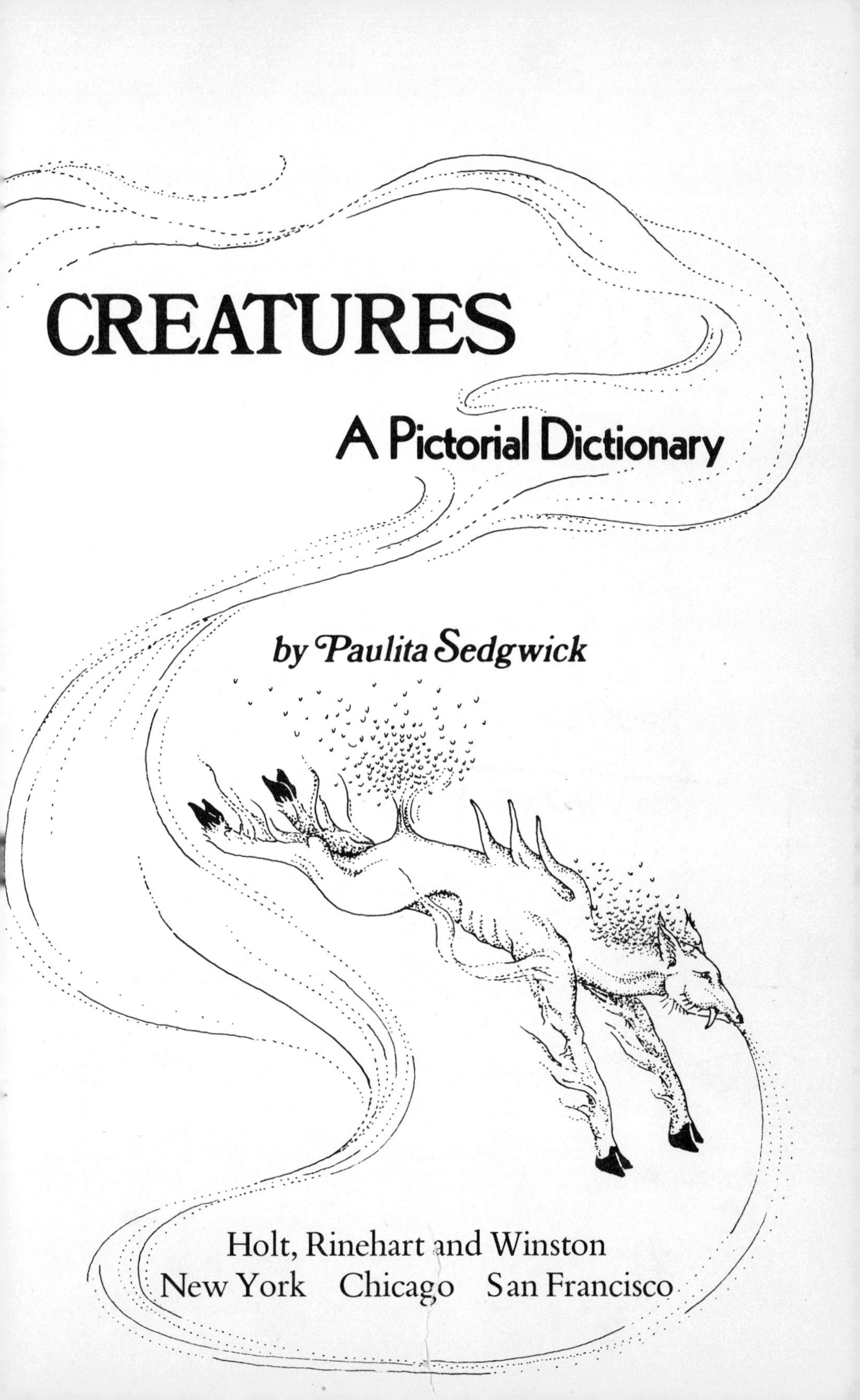

CREATURES

A Pictorial Dictionary

by Paulita Sedgwick

Holt, Rinehart and Winston
New York Chicago San Francisco

Published simultaneously in Canada by Holt, Rinehart
and Winston of Canada, Limited.
Library of Congress Cataloging in Publication Data
Sedgwick, Paulita.
Mythological creatures: a pictorial dictionary.
Brief alphabetically arranged entries
identify creatures of myth and folklore from various
countries including goblins, sylphs, werewolves, Punch
and Judy, Ravana, and others.
1. Animals, Mythical—Dictionaries—Juvenile
literature. 2. Mythology—Dictionaries—Juvenile
literature. 1. Mythology—Dictionaries I. Title.
GR825.S42 200'.4'03 74—8004
0-03-012946-X

Printed in the United States of America
First Edition

With all the magical beings who are different from the rest, to whom I dedicate this book, I share these twelve secrets:

- *To see magic, look out of the corner of your eye.*
- *Amulets will avert evil, talismans will bring good luck.*
- *If you are misled by fairies and find it hard to resist them, turn your clothes inside out and the fairies will go away.*
- *Eat neither fairy food nor in the world of the dead, or you will never again be able to return to your own world.*
- *Evil spirits can rarely cross running water, even if they themselves are watery.*
- *To call a wind, whistle.*
- *To make plants grow, sing.*
- *Do not be deceived by appearances. Demons often arrive in disguise.*
- *Garlic and crosses protect from evil, but good thoughts are the strongest defense.*
- *Beings without a soul cast no shadow.*
- *The moment you stop chasing your shadow, it will follow you faithfully.*
- *Never look back.*

Bold italic type at head of entry — See the entry referred to in **Bold Roman** type within the text for an illustration or further information.

MYTHOLOGICAL CREATURES

Acephali are headless people whose faces look out of their chests. Some lucky ones do have heads, but the heads are removable and can be carried under the arm. It is said that at one time the Acephali were perfectly normal, but they had the audacity to rebel against the gods. To punish their impudence and, as it were, cut them down to size, the gods decapitated them, and they have lived headless ever since.

Afrit, most powerful of Arabian **Djinn,** may appear in any shape, but, whether as camel or wind, they are always wicked.

Aglaia is one of the three charming **Graces.**

Alberich, the Teutonic **Dwarf** king, was guardian of the fabulous Nibelung treasure.

Al Burak, Arabian symbol of purity, is a marvelous, lady-faced mule with flowing peacock plumes. One night, she woke the Prophet Mohammed who, in his surprise, knocked over a glass of water. Mounting her, they flew from Mecca to Jerusalem and on through the seven heavens to speak to the angels. Finally at home again, the spilled water had not yet reached the floor. Such is the mystery of time!

Alchemists are mystical and austere scientists. Inventors of chemistry, they spend their lives experimenting in lonely laboratories, in hopes of finding the magical "Philosopher's Stone." The few who do finally find this stone can turn base metals into pure gold and, most important, they can prevent sickness and even death.

Aloadae were two **Giant** sons of the Greek sea god, Poseidon. Even while very young, they were quite enormous and grew at the rate of nine feet a year. They managed to escape from a bronze jar in which they had been imprisoned. Decidedly rambunctious and obnoxious, a perfect menace to the gods, they finally killed each other by mistake, much to everyone's relief.

Amalthea is the nanny goat who raised Zeus, father of Greek gods, whom she found abandoned on a mountainside. Later, to reward her, he placed her lovingly among the stars as the constellation Capricorn.

Amazons, traditionally from the Greek "amazos," meaning "breastless," were warrior women who cut off their right breasts so that it would not interfere with their archery. No man was allowed to stay more than nine days in the Near Eastern land of this all-female race. The Amazon area of South America was also believed to be inhabited by a race of fighting maidens.

Amphisbena (Greek for "to go both ways") is a strange little dragon-snake with a menacing head at each end of its body. It can move swiftly in either direction by clutching one head with the other and bowling along like a cart wheel. Its skin lies in flabby, scaly folds, and its beady eyes, although seemingly fierce, are dreadfully short-sighted. It can usually be found grubbing about in garbage dumps, looking for ants to eat.

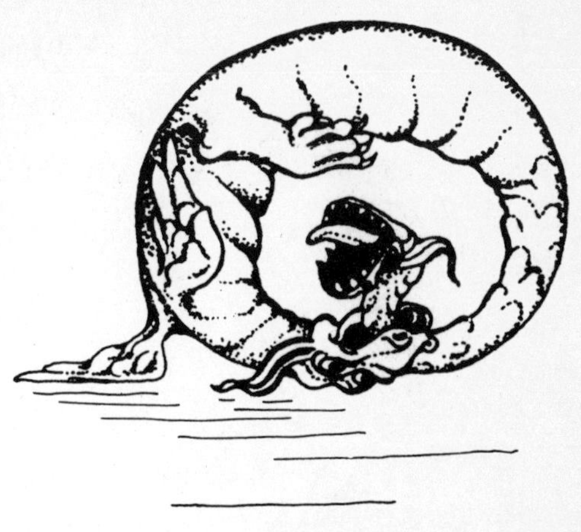

Amphitrite, the sweet **Nereid,** was loved by Poseidon, Greek god of the sea. He would ride to woo her mounted on a **Dolphin,** and, when she consented to marry him, he delightedly placed his Dolphin among the stars. To his young bride, he gave a golden palace beneath the waves.

Androsphinx, or Sphinx, is the male-headed lion of Egypt as opposed to the female **Sphinx** of Greece. Symbol of the sun and of power, the Egyptian Sphinx silently guards the entrance to temples and tombs. The oldest is the great Sphinx of Gizeh, who observes the desert sands with wise and secret eyes.

Angels are the splendid and awesome messengers of God. They are made of light and transport themselves with the speed of a miracle, carrying out the will of their Lord. Now they have been divided into hierarchies of which only the two lowest orders, Angels and Archangels, have personal dealings with man.

Angiras, the Indian **Angels,** are winged messengers who fly to and fro between gods and men. For this reason, they are called "sons of the gods and fathers of men."

Antelopes were swift as a wink in medieval times. They could only be caught if they accidentally entangled their saw-shaped horns in a bramble bush. Siberians say their speed was due to their six legs. In fact, no living man could boast of ever having caught one until the Great Hunter of the Sky gathered up all the antelopes and slowed them down by cutting off two legs from each. That is why, nowadays, antelopes have only four legs.

Ants, big as dogs, with wings and sharp tusks, live in India. These giant ants burrow all night for gold, hauling it to the surface by day. The neighboring peasants live in terror of these fierce insects, but at night, while the ants are underground, they creep out to steal away the treasure.

Anubis is the jackal-headed Egyptian god of the dead. He watches over the careful preparation of the mummies and, when they are carried to their tombs outside the city, he protects them from the real jackals that prowl the moonlit desert night after night, howling hungrily for food.

Apis, the great black **Bull,** is lord of the Egyptian underworld. He lives most luxuriously in the ancient Egyptian city of Memphis, where he is highly respected.

Apsaras are the broad-hipped Indian water **Nymphs.** They are langourous maidens with red-tinted toes whose misty clothing billows out over the water as they dance.

Argus had at least one hundred eyes and never slept with more than two at a time. Because of this peculiarity, the Greek gods used him as a watchman, a job for which he was admirably suited. When he died, Hera, Queen of the Gods, set his many eyes in the tail of her pet peacock; there they keep watch to this day.

Arimaspians are a greedy race of one-eyed people living in Scythia. All their ingenuity and effort is spent trying to steal the carefully hoarded gold of their **Griffon** neighbors.

Arion was the proud stallion son of the Greek sea god, Poseidon. He inherited from his watery father the thundering speed of rushing waves. From his gentle Earth mother, Demeter, he was gifted with a human voice and two human legs.

Aspidodelone was a horrific sea monster, part tortoise and part whale. When Jonah was sucked into his cavernous belly, he exclaimed in surprise, as he slid and slimed through the vast darkness, that he seemed to be in Hell itself. Later, the Greeks called this monster and others similar to him, **Zaratan** the floating island, and shipwrecked sailors told terrible tales about him.

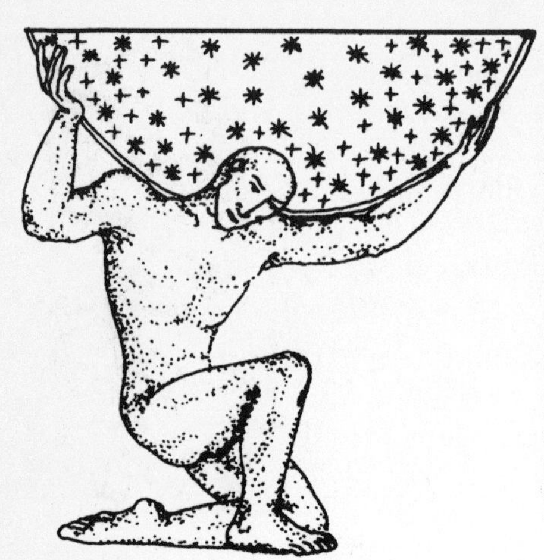

Atlas, a **Titan,** lives far beyond the Western Sea at the world's edge, in the land of sunset. There, he has a garden of golden fruit trees watched over by his pretty granddaughters, the **Hesperides.** He is also the father of the seductive nymph, **Calypso,** and of the seven **Pleiades.** The gods placed the whole of the starry sky on his shoulders and ordered him to hold it up like a canopy over our heads forever.

Atropos, "the one who cannot be restrained," is the last of the three **Fates.** It is she who, with her steady shears, cuts off each man's life thread when she decides his time has come to die.

Audhumbla is old German, meaning "dark void." In the beginning, before time began, warm winds from the south blew northward across the vast ice fields of space. From this billowing mist was born Audhumbla, the immense cosmic cow of Teutonic mythology, first of all living things.

Aurora Borealis, the Northern Lights, are called the "Merry Dancers" in Scotland. They are beautiful angels who were thrown out of Heaven long ago. Now they dance forever, trailing their rainbow scarves across the cold skies of the north.

Ba, in Egypt, is the soul which one day returns to the dead body.

Bacchae, like the Greek **Maenads,** were obsessed female devotees of the Roman wine god, Bacchus.

Badgers are mischievous fairy animals who bedevil the Japanese peasants for fun. The Badger can assume any shape, but, usually, it sits by the roadside disguised as a monk drinking rice wine and using its big belly as a drum.

Bahamut is the Arabian **Behemoth.** To them, he became an enormous, dazzlingly bright fish swimming on a bottomless sea. On his back, he carries the whole of creation.

Banshee is the Celtic fairy woman whose long, sad wail in the night warns of a death in the family. She is very beautiful, with streaming black hair and pale cheeks, but her woeful eyes are always red from weeping. Faithful and devoted to the family she watches, she tragically mourns the death of each one.

Baphomet, is supposedly a form of the **Devil** that the medieval Knights Templar were accused of worshiping. He is often represented as half male, half female, and crowned with crescent horns.

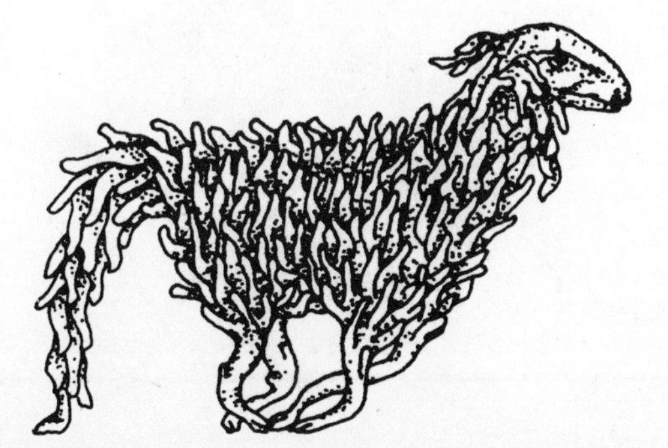

Barometz is a strange, mossy plant-animal, shaped like a lamb growing on four rooty legs. Wolves often feed on it. When picked, it is said to scream out in pain as drops of blood burst from its broken stems. This gentle animal is also called the Vegetable Lamb of Tartary.

Basilisk, or Cockatrice, the "Little King of Serpents," is a small but fearsome creature living in deserts laid waste by his poisonous stench. Hatched from a cock's egg brooded by a toad, he is part serpent and part rooster. His piercing, deadly eyes kill any creature they light on except the little weasel who is immune and attacks him fearlessly. The Basilisk himself would die were he accidentally to see his own reflection.

Bast was the cat-headed Egyptian goddess of fire. She represented the life-giving heat of the sun. As a pleasure goddess, she protected her followers from evils such as disease and famine while, in her splendid temple, people sang and danced in her honor. Because of her warm, happy nature, she was very much loved along the Nile Valley, where all cats were venerated for her sake.

Beelzebub, Lord of the Flies, is a popular name for **Lucifer,** King of Devils.

Bees, along with wheat and bananas, are the only things for which an origin cannot be found here on earth; so, they are said to have been given to man by ancient messengers from the planet Venus. Bees have been respected and even worshiped in many countries and ages because of their cleanliness and efficiency. As far back as the ancient civilizations of Egypt and Mesopotamia, the bee's sting was used as a powerful inoculation against disease and its wax as a purifier, while a spoonful of honey at bedtime brought sweet dreams.

Behemoth, the great primal beast, is stronger and mightier than all beasts together. Wading through the waters of chaos, he cools his hulking, steel-like body among delicate water flowers and gentle river winds. Some call him Ox because he feeds on grasses, some Hippopotamus, but he is greater and more durable than either.

Benu was the original **Phoenix** spoken of in Egypt. It symbolizes the sun which, having burned to glowing coals each evening in the west, rises fresh and new each morning.

Berserks, fearful warriors of the Norse god, Odin, rushed howling into battle wrapped in the skins of wolves and bears. They were so fierce and cruel that the peasants who fled from them in terror believed them to be ogres and monsters.

Bes was the Egyptian dwarf god of happiness. His home was far to the south, in the mysterious Land of Punt. He would, however, often appear when a child was born, to bring good fortune, like the **Fairy Godmothers** of later times. This deformed little god with his bandy legs and bulging eyes was so ugly and made such awful faces that the evil spirits would run away to hide in terror while all the good people laughed happily and danced in his honor.

Black Dandy Devil Dogs, alone or in packs, roam the bleak English moors on stormy nights or race with the clouds across the face of the moon. Their touch drives men mad, and their howls forbode death.

Blue Men of the Minch off the west coast of Scotland, are a race of rowdy mermen who cause treacherous storms at sea. Half men, half fish, they swim up the coast from Africa and are totally blue. Sailing is not safe when the Blue Men are about, and only a mariner who can riddle and rhyme can charm them into letting him pass.

Boars are sacred to Artemis, Greek goddess of the hunt. Once, a king out hunting gave chase to a wild boar. The animal fled, crying, "Spare me, I belong to the goddess!" Heedlessly, the king slew it and was immediately stricken with leprosy by the infuriated goddess. The king's sly mother presented the goddess with a marvelous gift, a boar with a human head. Inside it a music box repeated the words, "Spare me!" Enchanted, Artemis at once forgave the queen's insolent son and cured his leprosy.

Bogie, also called Boggart, Boggles, Cucui, or Coco, is a scary little sprite—dark and furry, with fiery red eyes—who lurks in cupboards and dark places. Only children can see him, but he is often heard rattling around, chuckling and getting into mischief.

Brownies are small, energetic, household creature. They wake up at night and finish all the chores—even taking care of the animals—and are especially good with bees. If you are lucky enough to have one, feed him on milksops, but never try to see him. Being shy, he will run away forever.

Bulls with Wings appear in many mythologies. Usually, they represent the constellation of the Great Bull, Taurus, symbol of fruitful energy. The Winged Bull of Saint Luke has such a profound knowledge of medicine that he can prevent even death itself.

Cailleach Bheur, the Blue **Hag** of Scotland, is the desolate old crone who brings winter. Wherever her staff falls, the ground freezes and no flowers ever again grow in that spot.

Caladrius was a pure white bird, highly prized in medieval Europe. Placed beside a sick man, the bird would look away if the patient had to die. If not, the Caladrius cured him by sucking up the disease and spitting it up into the sky.

Calliope is the **Muse** of Epic Poetry.

Calypso was a lovely **Nymph** who fell in love with the Greek adventurer, Odysseus. She lived on a lonely island called Ogygia, the "navel," because it lay in the center of the sea. Odysseus stayed with her for seven years and she promised him youth and immortality if he would stay forever. But homesick for his native land, the gods finally ordered her to let him go.

Capricorn is the sea goat of the zodiac. Once, **Pan,** frightened by the approach of the monster **Typhon,** changed himself into an animal and jumped into a lake to escape. At the moment of his transformation, he was half in and half out of the water; so, while his top became a goat, the bottom turned into a fish. This way the goat-fish Capricorn was born.

Carbuncle, in South America, is a small, rare creature with a lustrous and fiery jewel sprouting on its head. The medicinal and magical properties of this stone are greatly valued. **Dragons** and **Toads** grow similar, equally potent, gems.

Catoblepas is a black, scaly buffalo beast with pig's teeth and wings who lives in the Ethiopian mud flats. Its sleepy, half-closed eyes gaze out through a bristly mane, instantly striking dead any who see them. Fortunately, the Catoblepas is exceedingly lazy and always hangs his heavy head down close to the ground, so it is not difficult to avoid his deadly stare.

Cecrops, whose history is lost in shadows, was the first king of Athens. He had neither parents nor children and, like the Indian **Nagas,** was half man, half snake. A wise ruler, he established the way of government, invented writing, instituted marriage and burial and, generally, started his people on the road to civilization. He voted that Athena, the wise goddess who had given them the olive tree, should be their deity.

Centaurs, part man, part horse, are cruel immortal creatures who roam the hills of Thessaly. They brutally attack all who come near, and feast on raw flesh. Not all are destructive, however. Chiron, the wise and gentle centaur, trained many of the Greek heroes in the arts of music, medicine, and hunting. In the end he was accidentally wounded. The pain was so intense, that giving his immortality to **Prometheus,** Chiron was allowed to die. His image rose to heaven as the constellation Sagittarius.

Cerastes, the twisty snake, lies buried in the sand, showing only his four horns. Birds and small animals venturing to investigate the protruding spikes are instantly attacked by the wily serpent. These horns are also used by humans to detect poison hidden in food.

Cerberus is the three-headed watchdog who growls at the Gates of Death. All who enter throw honey cakes to distract his gnashing jaws. And his serpent tail darts venomously at any sly ghost trying to escape.

Chac are weepy-eyed, old Maya fertility gods. They ride the Mexican skies, herding clouds and pouring down rain. Shooting stars in the night are cigarette butts tossed from their heavenly haciendas.

Changelings are pale, frail fairy children left in exchange for a healthy human child. After stealing the real baby, the fairies touch its little eyes with their magic fingers so that it will see the world as they do and become fairy too.

Charites are the Greek counterparts of the lovely Roman **Graces.**

Chi Lyn is the wondrous Chinese **Unicorn.** He is like a deer with a single fleshy horn. He steps so gently, even the grass does not bow under him. Unwilling to harm living things, he eats fallen leaves and plants already dead. As the marvelous Chi Lyn appears only when a righteous ruler is born, the last one seen was in the days of Confucius. So, although they live a thousand years, they are very scarce.

Chimaera was the fantastic female monster who prowled the wild mountains of Asia Minor. She was lion in front, goat in the middle, and dragon behind, and with the head of each. After causing terrible damage with the volcanic fumes that puffed and billowed from her flaring nostrils, she was finally killed by young Bellerophon on his flying horse, **Pegasus.** Now we apply the name of the fire-spitting Chimaera to totally improbable ideas and absurdly fanciful images.

Cimmerians are a little-known mythical people sung about by the Greek epic poet, Homer. They live darkly in a fog-bound land where the sun never rises.

Cinomolgus, the Cinnamon Bird, makes its nest of cinnamon sticks. It builds them at the top of the tallest trees, too high up for people to climb. But men, being greedy, knock down the delicious nests by throwing rocks at them. Then they sell the precious sticks in the market.

Circe, wicked daughter of the Sun, is a powerful sorceress. She lives on a western island in a palace made of moonlight, and delights in practicing her black art by turning her visitors into animals. When the Greek, Odysseus, arrived, she transformed his men into swine and would have done the same to him had he not been given a magic herb to ward off her enchantments. Still, her spells were strong and her beauty great, and the hero stayed a year with evil Circe.

Clay Figurines placed by a **Shaman,** or Witch Doctor, beside his patient cure him by absorbing the illness into the clay itself.

Clio is the heroic **Muse** who inspires History.

Clotho is the **Fate** who slowly spins out the thread of life.

Cock of Dawn, the Heavenly Rooster of China, lives in a tree in the Land of Sunrise at the farthest edge of the world. His feathers are all of gold, and he stands proudly on his three legs. All the roosters of the earth are hatched from the eggs he lays, and their scarlet combs reflect the brilliant dawn. At daybreak, the Heavenly Rooster sings out his call that echoes around the world as his sons crow back.

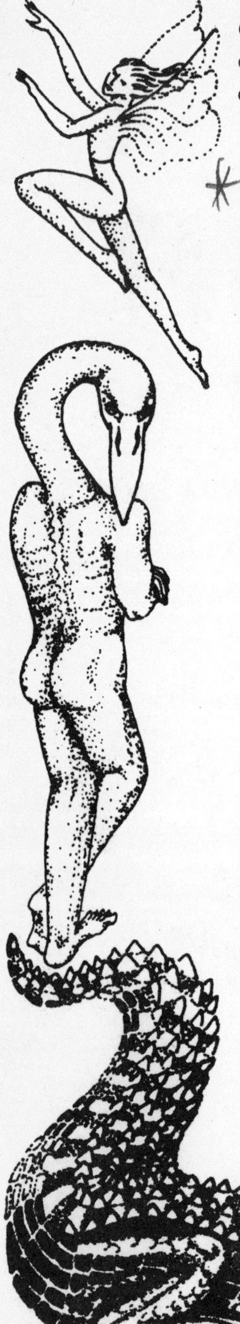

Corybantes were wild priests dedicated to the service of Cybele, the great corn goddess of Asia Minor. They celebrated her rites with the excessive madness shown by the **Maenads** in their worship of Dionysus.

Cottingley Fairies are pretty little nature sprites who inhabit the countryside around Cottingley Village in Yorkshire, England. In this village lived a young girl of thirteen called Elsie Wright and her cousin, Frances, who was only ten. Often they would spend the afternoon in the shady glen behind the cottage. There, beside the waterfall, they played with the fairies. When they told their parents what they had seen and done, they were given a terrible scolding for telling lies. So one day in 1917, the girls borrowed a camera and took actual photographs of their winged friends that now anyone may see.

Crane Men have human bodies and graceful bird heads.

Crocodiles have long been respected wherever they live. There is a lake now in Madagascar where, in olden days, a village used to stand. Long ago, a stranger came into that town asking for a drink of water. Only one woman stepped forward to give it to him. For her kindness, the stranger, who was really a powerful magician, warned her to quickly leave the village. When she had escaped, he turned the whole place into a lake and all the inhospitable inhabitants into crocodiles. Now, the surviving woman's descendants live in a new village near the lake and every year offer sacrifices to their crocodilian relatives.

Crocotta, born of a hyena and a lioness, is a ferocious animal living in the wilds of India and Ethiopia. His mouth stretches open in a horrible grin from ear to ear, revealing one long, continuous tooth. His back is also one unjointed bone so that he cannot bend, but must turn right around in order to look behind himself. He roams deserted places howling at the moon in a curiously human-sounding voice.

Cyclops are the immense sons of the earth and the sky. They have only one eye, placed right in the middle of their foreheads. Aggressive and fierce, these giants live in caves high in the mountains, where they forge thunderbolts and stir up terrible storms.

Cynocephali are dog-headed men who live on various remote islands. In China, there is a reverse creature, a dog with a man's head. Whenever he sees humans, laughing uproariously he summons a typhoon to blow them all away.

Daemon is an invisible but ever-present spirit who protects and advises like the **Guardian Angel** of the Christians. Each man at birth is given a Daemon by Zeus, Father of the Greek Gods. This lofty spirit guides and inspires him throughout his life. It is not evil and has nothing to do with what we call demons.

Dagon is the ancient fish god of the Assyrians. Although he is represented as half man, half fish, he is an earth god who oversees the fertility of the planting season and the fruitfulness of the harvest.

Demons and **Devils** are evil beings who delight in tempting people to do wicked things. Some assume strange, hideous, goatlike shapes—with horns, tails, and burning, red eyes—while others can appear quite beautiful. But even the prettiest have ugly shadows lurking behind their faces. The most dangerous, however, are the demons who are invisible when they do their molesting. Country people say that if a devil offers a man gold he may take it, if he wishes. But the gold will turn into withered leaves as soon as the Evil One turns his back.

Djinn are Arabian spirits, usually, but not always, evil. They were made of black fire eons before man came into the world. They whirl around the desert as wild dark clouds or writhing smoky winds. A sufficiently powerful wizard can command the Djinn to serve him, but should his strength fail, they will whisk him away to disaster.

Dolphins, protectors of man, may be his brothers. When mighty Atlantis sank, half the inhabitants fled to neighboring lands to study technology; these are man's ancestors. The rest, taking to the sea, became refined metaphysicians; these are now Dolphins. Mysteriously wise, even Apollo, the Greek **Sun,** became a Dolphin to found his oracle at Delphi.

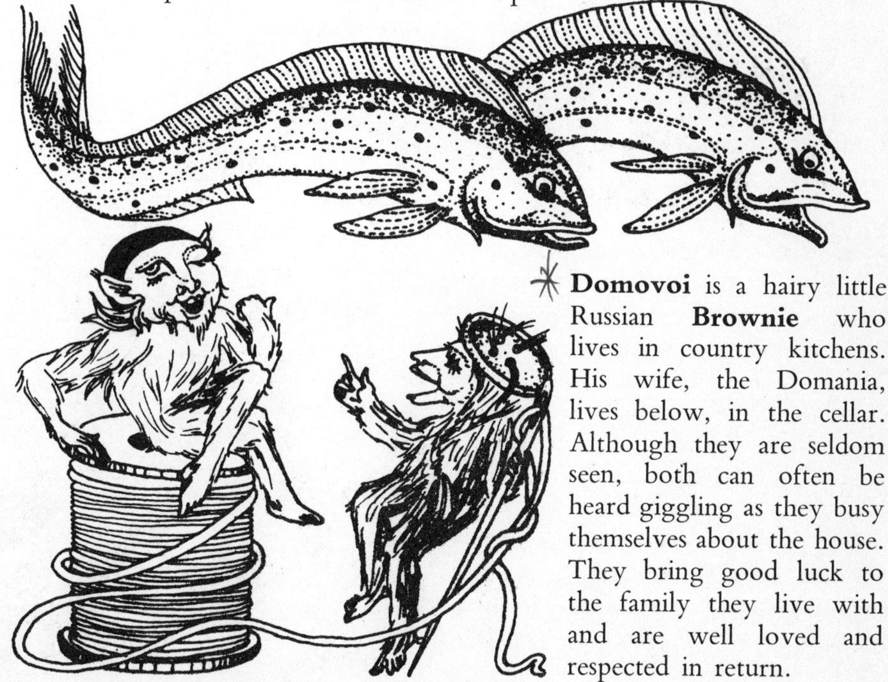

Domovoi is a hairy little Russian **Brownie** who lives in country kitchens. His wife, the Domania, lives below, in the cellar. Although they are seldom seen, both can often be heard giggling as they busy themselves about the house. They bring good luck to the family they live with and are well loved and respected in return.

Dracs are evil European river spirits. Unable to nurse their own children, they lure human women into doing it for them. Floating on the surface disguised as golden rings, they wait for a woman to try to catch them. Then they instantly pull her down into the water.

Dragons are huge, scaly, serpentine animals. Most have leathery wings, but their flight is so cumbersome that they prefer to ravage the countryside on foot, destroying every living thing in sight with their cruel claws and flaming breath. Though powerful, dragons have become rare since so many have been defeated by heroes.

Dryads are the **Nymphs** of the forest. Normally, they are gentle and shy, but if they feel that their trees are in danger, they become fiercely protective. The Dryads that actually form part of their trees are called **Hamadryads.**

Dwarves are gnarled little men who live in caves and underground passages. They are selfish and greedy, digging up gold and precious stones which they hoard just for the pleasure of fondling their treasures. If a man accepts a gift from a dwarf, he will soon pay in sorrow. Despite their lack of imagination and gnarled, twisted fingers, dwarves can make exquisite jewelry and magical weapons.

Eagle, conqueror of the air, represents the soul on its flight to Heaven. When he grows old, the Eagle soars to the highest peak of the sky and plunges down three times into a fountain of sunrise. As he dives, his feathers start to glisten and his body again grows young. In this way, like the soul, he is reborn. One of the largest Eagles is a Teutonic one living in the far north. All the winds of Heaven are stored under his wings and bluster out whenever he flies.

Earthquake Beetle, the Jinshin-Mushi of the Japanese, is a gigantic, scaly beetle with ten shaky, hairy spidery legs and an angry expression on its dragon face. It lives underground, balancing the island of Japan precariously on its back. When it sneezes, hiccups, or in any way shifts its position, the whole land trembles above him. That is said to be the cause of earthquakes in that country.

Echidna, half woman and half serpent, sprang from the black water of chaos that boiled underground at the beginning of the world. From her scaly, loathsome body sprang many of the vile monsters that were later to become famous. Among her children were the impossible **Chimaera,** the riddling **Sphinx,** the **Hydra,** and the fierce dogs, **Cerberus** and **Orthros.**

Echo was a pretty little nymph. She was lively, gay, and entertaining, but she had one fault: she never stopped talking. As a punishment, the Greek gods took away her power of speech, allowing her only to repeat what she heard. This enforced silence made Echo so sad that her body dwindled away and vanished, leaving only her sweet, pale voice to haunt the hills and empty palace halls.

Elementals are the spirits who populate each of the four elements of which all things are made: **Salamanders** are the Elementals of Fire; **Sylphs,** of Air; **Undines,** of water; and **Gnomes,** of the Earth. Each Elemental is made entirely of the element in which it lives.

Ellerwomen are Scandinavian fairy women who can sometimes be seen dancing in ruined buildings or other abandoned places to music played by unseen hands. If a passerby sees them, he is surely drawn by their beauty to join their dance, only to discover as he wraps his arm about her waist that the Ellerwoman's back is as hollow as her heart.

Elves, in Teutonic myth, used to mean any nature spirit whether good or evil. Since then, the word has come to apply only to the Light Elves who are tiny beings, bright as sunlight sparkling on the water. They flutter from flower to flower filling them with nectar and pollen. At dawn, they lay jeweled nets of dew across the grass and pinch the birds to wake and sing in the new day. Not very smart, thinking tires them, but they do nature's delicate work better than the wise men.

Empusae are the abominable servants of Hecate, goddess of the dark of the **Moon.** Whatever shape they assume, whether dog, cow, or maiden, they can always be recognized by their bronze sandals. They descend on travelers late at night or lure a lonely man into a fond embrace, and then eat him, leaving only his bones by the roadside.

Ercinee are German birds whose phosphorescent feathers shine in the dark. Their South American cousin, Alicanto, acquires his brilliance from eating quantities of gold ore. The metal lies so heavily in his stomach, that instead of flying, he waddles along the ground. Cucuio, a more friendly bird, allows men to work by the light of the lamps that glow brightly from his forehead and wings.

Eumenides, the "kindly ones," is the ironic Greek name for the **Furies.**

Euterpe is the **Muse** of wild music and sylvan flutes.

Evil Eye is not a horrible eyeball floating through space. It is a malefic look cast by a **Magician** trying to curse someone. The Evil Eye can be averted by wearing certain charms, such as blue glass beads. By attracting the Magician's eye as he speaks his malediction, these pretty objects draw the evil into themselves instead.

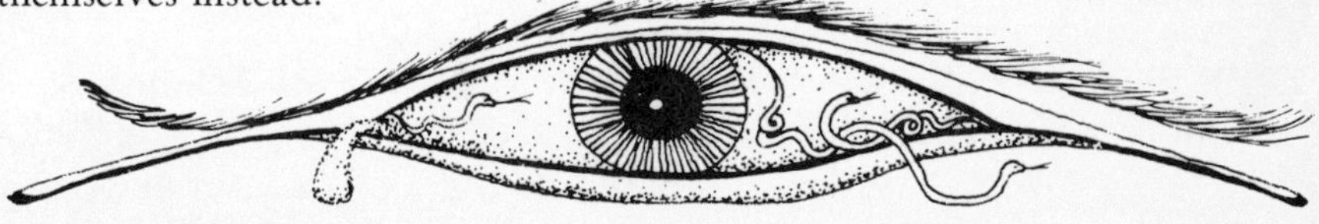

Fafnir, in Teutonic mythology, was a giant who transformed himself into a fearful dragon in order to guard an enormous cache of hidden treasure. After many adventures, the hero, Sigurd, killed him and, by eating the dragon's magical heart, acquired the power of both speaking and understanding the mysterious song language of birds.

Fairies, the Great **Shee** of Ireland are a taller and far nobler race than man. They cross easily between the barriers of space and time, making things seem to be what they are not. Noble and graceful, theirs is a world of illusion where there is neither right nor wrong. Dressed in white and green, they dance in magic circles on moonlit fields or woodland clearings. Sometimes, they go riding on great white horses hung with silver bells.

Fairy Godmothers are gentle **Fairies** who visit a newborn child to give him gifts. They bring marvelous, long-lasting things that will always be useful, such as beauty, generosity, or wisdom. Sometimes, a wicked fairy, hearing of the birth and angry at not having been invited, bursts in on the ceremony. She also brings a gift, but hers is a wretched gift of selfishness or vanity that will secretly poison the child's life.

Fates are the three wizened old women who give advice to the gods and allot to each man his destiny. Like the **Fairy Godmothers,** they appear when a child is born. Lachesis is the Fate who decides what that life is to be. Clotho spins the life into existence day after day as the child grows to adulthood and old age. And when the person's time comes to die, "unrestrainable" Atropos cuts off the silver lifeline.

Fauns are tricky little creatures with goat legs and pointy ears. They romp and play through Roman forests and countrysides, making mischief among the woodland creatures and having a world of fun. They are similar to the Greek **Satyrs,** but not as obnoxious.

Feng is the three-legged **Phoenix** of the Chinese. He and his wife are the birds of eternal love. They are radiantly beautiful to look upon and live forever in the heart of the shining sun.

Fenrir is the wolf son of Loki, destructive fire god of the Norsemen. At the end of the world, he will leap up from the earth in one bound and gobble up the sun.

Fiends, the hated ones, are the treacherous **Devils** of old England.

Fisher King is the mysterious lord of the fabled Isle of Avalon. To reach his remote castle, one must cross a vast chasm spanned by a terrifyingly narrow bridge which widens of its own accord once the attempt is made. There, he guards the sacred Grail out of which Jesus Christ drank at his Last Supper. Only those pure in mind and heart may look on this holy object, the sight of which cleanses the soul and brings infinite peace.

Flute Player was a hunchback who led the Indian people into America many hundreds of years ago. As he went, he drew seeds from the hump on his back, scattering them on the fertile ground. Then he played sweet, mysterious music while the plants grew in happy profusion from sea to sea making America a paradise for his Indian tribes to live and grow wise in.

Foxes, in the Orient, are illusive creatures, shifting shape at will. Marvelous enchanters, the greatest are distinguished by their nine bushy tails. Often assuming lovely, maidenly forms, they lure men into awful situations. But to friends, they bring abundant treasure and protection.

Frankenstein was a monster-man made by the mad Doctor Frankenstein in his laboratory. Escaping from his maker, the huge man set out to explore the countryside, causing havoc among the people who were terrified by his ungainly and inhuman aspect. Clumsily attempting to make friends, he accidentally killed the very ones he loved.

Frost Giants are the Teutonic **Jotuns.** They are the hoary giants of frozen fjord and snowbound mountains, mammoth iceberg men of the northern seas.

Fuaths are evil, Scottish water creatures. They are green all over with yellow horse manes and tails. To compensate for having no noses, their eyes are extra sharp. They creep about underwater, nabbing unsuspecting swimmers with their webbed toes and pulling them under to drown.

Furies are hellish women who sprang from the earth. Their duty is to severely punish any unnatural act, such as the sun rising at night or a man's extreme cruelty. Relentless and pitiless, they enforce nature's laws.

Gandayaks, among the Iroquois Indians, are small spirits who live in the river and take care of it. They clear the ice away in the spring and lead the fish upstream to spawn. In the autumn, they rush the fallen leaves to sea and keep the river clean.

Gandharvas are Indian celestial beings. Some say they are like **Centaurs**—part man, part horse—to represent their licentious ways and generative powers. Others believe they are half man, half bird, symbolizing their divine knowledge and spiritual aspect. Because, when a man dies, it is the Gandharvas who guide his soul to its next incarnation. They live in marvelous cities in the sky where they guard the Soma, elixir of life and power which they distribute to the gods. Accomplished musicians, they can usually be found cavorting with the amorous **Apsaras.**

Ganesha is a fat little Indian god with four arms, yellowish skin, and an elephant head with a single tusk. One of the many legends of his birth tells that there was a time when many mediocre people were getting into Heaven by making holy pilgrimages. The gods were worried that Heaven was getting too crowded, while Hell was quite empty. So one goddess created Ganesha, who would make men so eager for wealth that they would forget to make pilgrimages. Well loved, he is always invoked before new projects are started, and, as the god of learning and logic, he removes obstacles and explains things clearly and easily.

Gargoyles are ugly little monstrosities carved or sculpted onto the outside of buildings to frighten away evil spirits. They are often attached to the eaves of the roof and act as water-spouts, spitting the falling rain away from the windows, out into the street.

Garmr, the vicious dog-guardian of the underworld, is the **Cerberus** of Teutonic mythology.

Garuda is the golden vulture man of India. Spreading his red wings, he flies faster than the wind, carrying Vishnu, the gentle blue-skinned god, on his back. Garuda, whom the gods made immortal, knows the essence of the whole universe and is godlike in his ways.

Genie is one Arabian demon, while **Djinn** are many. It is easier to control them one at a time, but even that is hard. It is said that the shooting stars are God's warning arrows fired at them.

Gerion was a monster-man who was finally killed by the Greek hero, Hercules. Three bodies, three heads, and wings joined to form his grotesque figure. He was the proud owner of the two-headed dog, **Orthros,** and also of a large herd of bright-red cattle who found nothing more delicious than human flesh.

Ghosts are tormented spirits of the dead who wander restlessly because of some task left unfinished during their lives. If a man dies by treachery, his ghost may seek revenge. Or, he may come back to protect a loved one or a hidden treasure. Ghosts may appear in their former human shape, but having no substance, they don't have to keep their feet on the ground and can walk through walls if they want to. The only way to put a ghost to rest is by taking vengeance on his enemies for him and praying for the peace of his soul.

Ghouls are the **Ghosts** that haunt graveyards.

Giants were the first men to walk on earth. Their father was the sky, their mother the earth. Huge as mountains and gnarled as the withered tree trunks they use as clubs, they have been driven to the most remote corners of the world by the smaller, smarter race of men that came after them. Now the giants live in musty caves, eating whatever they can catch and terrifying any humans that pass their way. Most of the time, they are quite lonely and entertain themselves by tossing large boulders about and complaining of hard times.

Gnomes are **Elementals,** or spirits, living in and composed entirely of the Element Earth. Dressed in brown hooded clothes, these gnarled little dwarves have red eyes and runty legs. As earthy spirits, they know where veins of precious ore run and where the brightest diamonds lie hidden under eons of buried coal. They guard mountains, cliffs, and caves, and carefully direct the changing surface of the earth.

Goblins are nimble, thievish old men of various sizes with distorted features, such as square toes or three noses. Their voices sound like mud squishing under a rock or chalk dust filtering through a crack. They are earthy creatures—dim-witted, and clumsy—and can be awfully cruel if the mood so takes them. Stealing is part of their nature; so, if there is nothing else to take, they might just steal each other.

Gog and Magog are the mighty **Giant** grandsons of Noah. Chiefs of violent and barbaric Aryan hordes, they sweep down periodically on the gentle countries to the south, plundering and gathering slaves. But one day, the Children of God will conquer them and their graves will occupy the whole length of a valley and take seven months to dig.

Golden Fleeced Ram carried the grandchildren of the wind away from their wicked stepmother. The girl fell off along the way but the boy, arriving safely, sacrificed the ram to the gods in gratitude. He hung its Golden Fleece on a tree, where Jason found it many years later.

Golem is a hulking figure shaped of mud and clay by a wise rabbi. When the Holy Name of God is placed under its tongue or on its forehead, it is animated into a sort of senseless, speechless life.

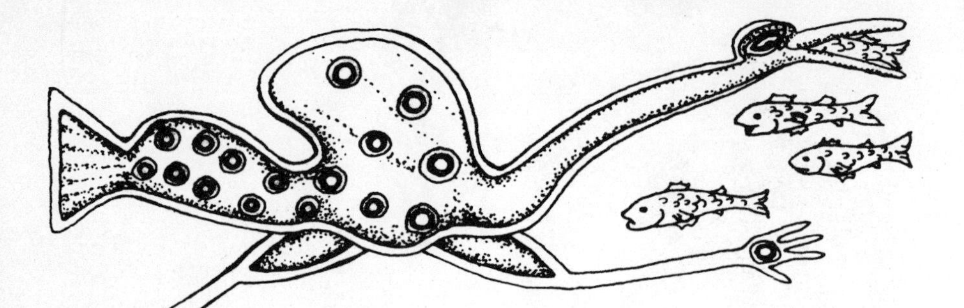

Gonafo, the great fish-eating bird, is king of all the magical creatures of Dahomey, West Africa.

Gopis, the silver-eyed cowgirls, are buxom, frolicking nymphs of Hindu mythology. They attend to their herds, but tend more to chase after their handsome, blue-skinned Lord Krishna.

Gorgons are three monstrous, snaky-haired sisters, from whom one look turns men to stone. All are immortal except for the youngest, **Medusa.**

Graces are three lovely sunbeam nymphs. They ripen fruit, cause flowers to bloom, and bring gentleness and joy to the heart. They accompany any person who wishes for them, bringing to humans their happy gifts of kindness, generosity, and delightful conversation.

Graiae are three horrendous hags, sisters of the snake-haired **Gorgons.** Old and decrepit even at birth, they are blind except for one eye, which they share. When Perseus came hunting the Gorgons, he waited until the Graiae could not see as they passed the eye among them. Then, snatching it from the fumbling hands, he refused to give it back until they told him where their ugly sisters lived.

Grant is a terrible red-eyed horse. At the witching hours of noon and twilight, he runs through English village streets raised upright on his two hind legs. He is an evil omen, with disaster following close behind.

Gremlins are the **Brownies** of airplanes. They are mischievous little creatures who scramble into the engine to drink the gasoline and send out fiery sparks to scare the pilot. Luckily, they do not get along with carrier pigeons and will not get aboard if the pilot takes one with him.

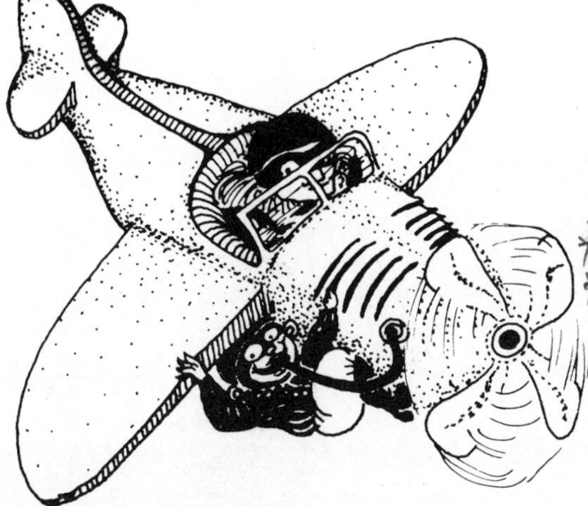

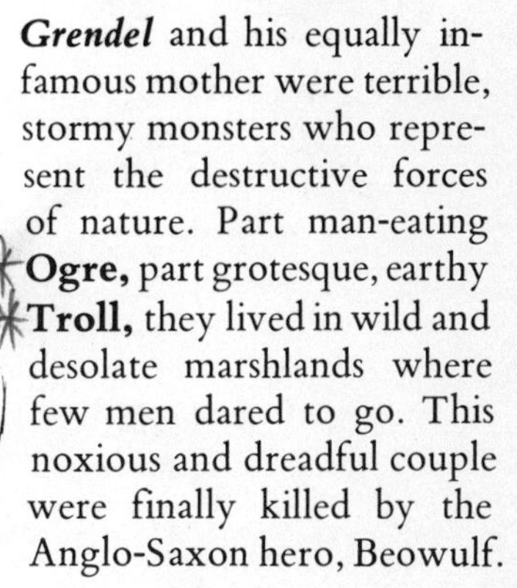

Grendel and his equally infamous mother were terrible, stormy monsters who represent the destructive forces of nature. Part man-eating **Ogre,** part grotesque, earthy **Troll,** they lived in wild and desolate marshlands where few men dared to go. This noxious and dreadful couple were finally killed by the Anglo-Saxon hero, Beowulf.

Griffons are huge, powerful beasts, part winged eagle, part bold lion. Renowned for their courage, the griffons guard the golden mountains. They spend most of the time repelling the attacks of the greedy, one-eyed **Arimaspians.**

Guardian Angel is a great and beautiful **Angel** that helps and protects a person from the moment of birth all through his life. Every person has an angel. Although good, wise, and ready to be of help, the angel is seldom consulted. The Guardian Angel is thought to be a person's higher self, the image of what each person could be if he or she were nearer perfection.

Gullinbursti, the "gold-bristled" is a mechanical boar, molded of solid gold. It can travel at will through air, earth, or water with equal speed. Made in the depths of the earth by nimble-fingered dwarves, Gullinbursti belongs to handsome Frey, one of the ancient Teutonic **Vanir,** or wind gods.

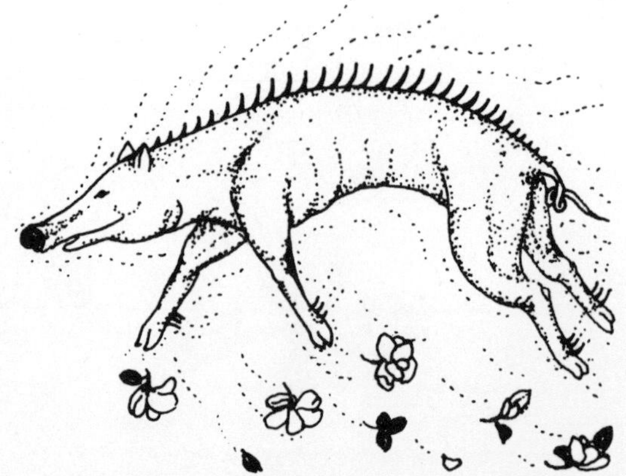

Hags are supernatural crones, wrinkled old women, bent and shriveled, but strong and relentless as iron or ice. Wherever they go, winter soon follows. Their eyes, wrapped in dark mist, pity neither man nor beast. With icy breath, they wither the heart and freeze leaves on the trees, for they represent winter, old age, and the cold, dying moon.

Hamadryads are the **Dryads,** or spirits, who actually live in the tree itself. Its bark is their clothing, its leaves and flowers, their decoration. Every tree and bush has its Hamadryad and, when it dies, she dies with it. Whenever a tree is felled, the high-pitched wail of the dying nymph causes all the trees of the forest to shiver and sigh, although it is too fine a voice for mortal ears to hear.

Hanuman, the monkey divinity, is the son of a monkey queen. The wind, his father, gave him his ability to fly and his great speed. When he was born, he was so hungry that he would have eaten the sun, thinking it was a large yellow fruit, had the gods not stopped him. For his devoted loyalty and service to Rama, hero of the Indian epic, "Ramayana", he was offered any reward he chose. He asked to live as long as the memory of Rama's exploits. In this way, he humbly became immortal.

Hare of Jade is the title of the rabbit that lives in the **Moon.** Once the greatest of the Chinese gods, the August Emperor of Jade, called for food. As a gesture of religious devotion Buddha, incarnated as a hare at the time, hopped into a pot and offered himself to be eaten. As a reward for his self-sacrifice, the gods sent his soul to live under the Cassia tree on the moon, where he forever mixes the Elixir of Immortality.

Harpies are wild and furious Greek bird goddesses who fly on stormy wings across cloud-battered skies. Screaming shrill cries into the wind, they whirl earthward to steal the food right from under people's noses. Trailing filth and a disgustingly evil stench, they spread famine, pestilence, and death across once-fertile land.

Hathor is the great celestial cow-goddess of the ancient Egyptians. She is the gentle mother who gives life with her milk. She lives at the edge of the great desert, perched in a sycamore tree. When a person dies, she is the protective guide who, meeting his soul, carries it safely into the other world. If the person has led a particularly holy life she allows him to climb the long ladder up to Heaven. Seven Hathors, like **Fairy Godmothers,** plan each child's life at birth.

Heads with neither necks nor bodies can be found flying, roaring, and rolling through the folklore and mythologies of the world.

BIG HEADS of the Iroquois Indians are great, hairy heads that rampage across stormy skies among lowering clouds. With lightning flashing from their eyes and thunder billowing from their ears, they tear across the windswept country, uprooting trees and snatching away people and animals in their sharp clawed hands.

CABEZUDOS are huge, Spanish heads with protruding eyes and tongue. Every year, they parade through the streets to devour small children and spit them out again.

CHONCHON, in South America, is a winged head who flies about on dark nights. It can only be seen by powerful magicians. But if they attack or in any way molest the Chonchon, thousands of its brothers swarm to its aid.

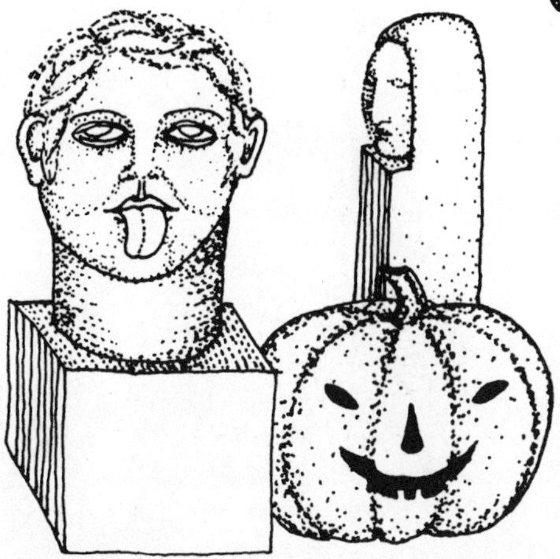

ORACULAR HEADS are made in many different ways: some are mummified human heads, some are made of marble or bronze, and one was carved like a jack-o'-lantern out of a pumpkin. They are made and frequently consulted by magicians. Often inscribed with magical inscriptions, the Oracular Heads can tell of times past and times to come if the right incantations are spoken over them.

Hecatoncheires is the Greek word meaning the "ones with a hundred hands." They are brothers both of the **Cyclops** and of the **Titans.** Monstrous and tempestuous sons of the Earth, they each have fifty heads and, as their name implies, a hundred arms. When they wrestle each other, the ground trembles for miles around; when they race, thunderclouds and whirlwinds darken the sky.

Heidrun is Odin's goat, whose sweet, heavy milk nourishes all the Norse gods.

Hermaphrodite was the beautiful son of Hermes, the messenger, and Aphrodite, goddess of love. Wild and free as a silver wind, he roamed the wooded mountains. One day, as he cooled himself in a lake, the lake's nymph, seeing him, fell deeply in love. Winding him in her watery arms, she covered him with kisses, while the timid boy tried to escape. Desperately, the nymph called on the gods to unite them. Instantly, their two bodies melted inseparably into one: half male, half female.

Hesperides, fairer than the golden clouds of dawn, are the three bright-haired, smiling daughters of the evening star. They live beyond the ocean in the land of sunset where they are said to guard trees filled with golden apples. But the girls, between chattering and laughing, ate so many of the apples themselves that a dragon was sent to live there, too, and keep the pretty guardians away from their trees.

Hippocampus, the sea horse, used to be as large as a real horse, with flashing hooves on his forelegs and a long mane streaming down over his scaly lower half. But long years of living in the sea, cavorting in its waves, and weathering its storms, have slowly worked a change: the Hippocampus has shriveled into the delicate fairy-sized horse with long snout and fishy tail whose desiccated skeleton can sometimes be found washed up on lonely beaches.

Hippogriff is the improbable offspring of a mare and a **Griffon.** Improbable because Griffons detest horses, and seldom go near them. It is probable that the only Hippogriff ever seen is the one mentioned by the medieval Italian writer, Ariosto, who said it lived in icebound mountains in the north. It has the horse hind parts of its mother, and the winged and feathered front of its Griffon sire.

Hob, or Hobgoblin, is not like a wicked **Goblin** at all. Quite the contrary. He is a raggedy, furry little hearth spirit who looks after the kitchen and children when no one else is around. He is a wilder version of a **Brownie.** Although the Hob is rather dirty and hairy, he surely can do some lovely magical tricks to make the baby laugh. Sometimes, a bridge or a pond has its sprightly Hobgoblin to look after it.

Homunculi are miniature, but perfectly formed and proportioned, men. Great **Alchemists** have been known to make them in laboratory test tubes. Homunculi are wonderful creatures with strange and marvelous powers. They learn, as plants do, without ever having been taught. Having great knowledge of nature and other secret things normally hidden from humans, they are able to, and do, communicate these truths to their makers.

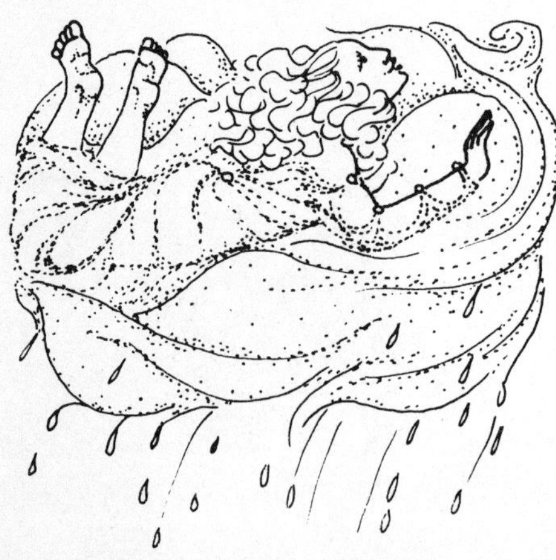

Horae are three lithe and lovely divinities of the changing seasons. They bring sweet rain in the flowering spring and, in the fall of the year, they paint the golden corn. They protect children and try to keep peace between men. They also control the Gates of Heaven, blocking its entry with a fat, white cloud or opening it by blowing the cloud away. Each holds a seasonal symbol: a flower, an ear of corn, and a vine.

Horses are often engendered by Wind and Water. Mares who love the wild West Wind bear stormy colts, swift as arrows but short-lived. Sometimes, a proud black stallion gallops out of the ocean, attracted by an earthly mare. Restless as their sire, their foals go back to the sea.

Horus, the falcon-headed Egyptian sky god, is called Lord of the Heavens and Ruler of all Egypt. In his right eye, he holds the sun, in his left eye, the moon. As god of light and justice, he spends most of his time avenging the murder of his father, Osiris. Osiris had been lured into a coffin and later cut to pieces by his own brother, Set, ass-eyed god of evil darkness. So Horus, the faithful daylight sky, and Set, the tricky night, spend the eons fighting on the battlegrounds of the universe.

Houris are voluptuous maidens living in the Moslem paradise. Seventy-two of them, with soft, dark, welcoming eyes, attend each dying man worthy of Heaven. Fairer than summer moons, they pour endless cups of wine and serve sweet fruits of every kind.

Hrimfaxi is the frosty-maned steed of night. He gallops wildly across the sky until, at dawn, the froth falling from his bit spatters the earth with morning dew.

Hulderfolk are the "hidden folk" of Scandinavia. Marvelously beautiful, these **Fairy** people are gracefully human in shape, except for their long monkeylike tails. They often marry mortals and, losing their tails, become as human beings. The children of a mortal man and a hidden lady are fortunate indeed: they are born with the power to see wonderful things, both past and future, things that ordinary people cannot know.

Humbaba, a vast mountain giant, was guardian of the cedar forest. His voice was like the roar of ice cracking in spring. Deep fires flickered in the hollows of his cavernous mouth and his breathing rumbled the earth. The Assyrian god-man, Gilgamesh, finally cut off his head.

Hydra of Lerna was a venomous serpent with nine human heads, one of which was immortal. Hercules, the Greek, was sent to kill it, and, as he chopped off each head, he sealed the neck stub with fire so it could not grow back. The last undying head he buried firmly under a rock, where it still lies grumbling.

Hyperboreans are a gentle, highly civilized and ancient people. They live on an island beyond Boreas, the north wind. Their air is made of feathers through which they drift softly, bathing their pale blue skin in the rays of the never-setting sun.

Ichthyocentaurs are rare, semi-divine creatures of the ocean. Wild and restless, the Ichthyocentaurs are part **Centaur,** part **Triton.** Their handsome human torsos rise above the water as they thrash the deep waves with their horses' hooves and dolphin tails.

Ikezuki is the miracle horse of Japan about whom many stories are told. Among his accomplishments is his remarkable ability to swim. While still a young colt, Ikezuki, wandering alone one day, bent his head to drink in a clear, dark pool. There in the still waters, he saw his own reflection. He neighed for joy, and, thinking it was his mother, leaped into the water to join her. He quickly realized that what he had seen was only an image, but kicking his legs, he was soon swimming happily.

Illuyankas, the Hittite dragon, went to dine with his enemy, the storm god. The god kept serving endless tasty tidbits and pouring rich flagons of sweet wine. Finally, quite besotted, the greedy dragon staggered back to his lair, only to find that he had grown too fat to squeeze inside. Then the wily Wind blew up and cut off his head.

Imps are horrid little **Devils.** Not quite grown up, they have a vivid imagination for inventing nasty jokes to play on unsuspecting humans.

Incubi are lusty, little demons that attach themselves to a sleeping woman's body. Sometimes disguised as a mole, sometimes as a birthmark, they grow large and beautiful at night. Sitting on the chest of their human victim, they bring strange dreams from which more demons like themselves are born. Their female counterparts are called **Succubi.**

Inkpot Monkey is a tiny creature with bright, red eyes and soft, black fur. In spite of being Chinese it loves the taste of India ink and will sit on the desk patiently waiting until some one leaves the inkpot unstoppered. Then it jumps up to the rim and drinks all that is left in the bottle. Afterward, climbing back down, he happily sleeps it off.

Innua are the Eskimo nature spirits. Each thing, whether it be vegetable, animal, or mineral, has its own small guardian Innua. Sometimes, the Innua of especially holy men are taken up to Heaven and turned into stars.

Jaculi are wicked vipers that spring like daggers from the shriveled trees of African deserts.

Janus, the earliest Roman god, has two faces, one young and one old, looking in opposite directions. As supervisor of all beginnings, he makes sure the sun rises daily and is invoked before every new undertaking. He is god both of the new day and of the new year, turning his old face to the past while his young one greets the future. Finally, as god of doorways, he looks both in and out: holding in one hand a key to open the gate and in the other a strong staff to beat away any unwelcome intruder.

Jormungard is a monstrous serpent thrown by Odin, father of Teutonic gods, into the Ocean. There he grew until his writhing body completely surrounded the world and his tail ended up in his mouth, like the **Ouroboros.** At the end of the world, he will devour the earth in one gulp, while his brother, the wolf, **Fenrir,** gobbles up the sun.

* **Jotuns** are the cold, ice-eyed Frost **Giants** of Teutonic mythology. They were driven back by the gods and heroes to the bitter hail-struck and snowbound lands at the top of the world. Far to the North, their frozen, scaly bodies glisten through the long dark months. Their helmets are crowned with curved horns that menace the night like glistening crescent moons rising behind the high peaks of their foreheads.

Ka, according to the people of ancient Egypt, is the spirit or personality of a man that lives on when the body dies. A little statue of the man's Ka was always buried with him. Sometimes magician-priests would take the Ka-statue of a wise man and, through various magical means, force it to actually speak, prophesying and advising.

Kachinas are supernatural beings who come from the western mountains to visit the Hopi Indians. They stay for half the year, dancing and bringing the children gifts. Some are fearsome spirits who, seeking those who have done wrong, whip them in punishment. All the Kachinas are able to bring rain, which is life itself, to the desert people.

Kappa is a terrible Japanese water demon. He looks like an ugly, pea-green monkey with a tortoise shell on his slimy back. In the top of his head is a bowl-shaped hollow which holds the secret waters of his powers. If he spills the water, he loses his magic. Although quite ludicrous looking, he is both dangerous and troublesome. Drowning children is his special fun, but, if none are available, he enjoys sucking on melons and cucumbers while waiting for a passing traveler to drag under water. Sometimes, he also teaches the delicate art of bone setting.

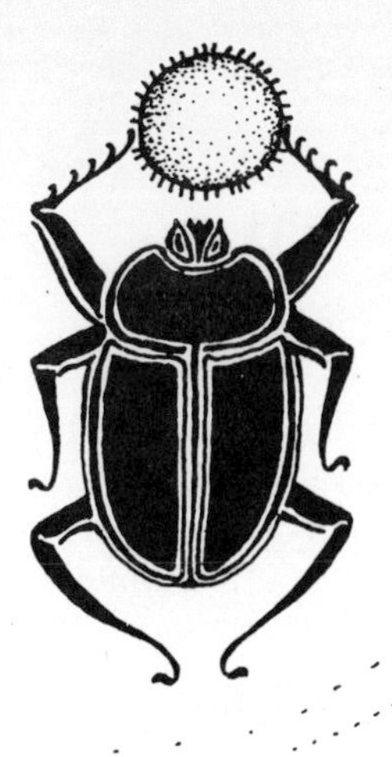

Khepri is the Egyptian scarab god of change, renewal, and eternity. God of dawn, he rolls the sun up over the horizon, bringing in each new day forever throughout time. He is represented as a scarab—hardiest of beetles—whose cockroach cousins still survive to prove that some things never change.

Kingmingoarkulluk is a tiny Eskimo divinity. He lives far out in the icy wastelands of the Arctic Circle and sings for joy whenever a human being comes into sight. He can be very helpful, if you can find him.

Knockers are sad, wan little men whose picking and tapping can be heard by Cornish miners deep inside the earth. The legend goes that they are the lost spirits of a group of Jews who were forced to work the tin mines a long time ago. The mine shaft caved in, imprisoning the unfortunate workers. Now, they help other miners by invisibly knocking to point out rich veins of ore and to warn of danger in the tunnels.

Kobolds are wrinkled old **Brownies** of the Germanic countries. They wear tall, pointed hoods and live in cellars or barns. A family is most fortunate to have one because he does a lot of house and yard work, but they must remember to give their Kobold a bowl of milk at the end of each day. If they forget, the little spirit takes his revenge with horrid tricks: He may whisk the stool away when the housewife goes to sit. And while she picks herself up, red-faced, from the floor, she will hear him giggling as he vanishes into a dark corner.

Kraken lies sleeping deep under the sea off the coast of Scandinavia. When he rises to the surface, his huge round body and myriad thrashing arms cause tremendous upheavals and whirlpools in the ocean for miles around. He is himself half a mile across and spits clouds of black ink into the surrounding water to hide himself from his enemies.

Krampus is a small, furry goblin with horns and a tail. At Christmas time in Austria, he trots alongside old Saint Nicholas, or **Santa Claus.** They fly in through the open windows of children's bedrooms to fill the waiting shoes with lovely surprises. The good Saint leaves sweet things and pretty shiny toys for the good boys and girls. While into the shoes of the naughty children, ugly little Krampus pours pebbles and lumps of coal. Sometimes, while Krampus is not looking, Saint Nick, who is so very kind, leaves a trinket even for the bad children in hopes that they will behave better next year.

Kujata is an enormous Moslem bull. He stands, straddling his four thousand legs on the slippery back of the giant fish, **Bahamut.** His myriad eyes, ears, noses, and mouths perceive all things, and he carries the world on his back.

Lachesis is the **Fate** who allots each man his destiny.

Ladon was a terrifying dragon who guarded the garden of the **Hesperides.** When he was killed by the Greek hero, Hercules, the gods placed him in the sky as the snaky constellation, "Serpens."

Lady of the Lake, or fair Nineve, as she is also called, is a strange and powerful queen. It was her hand that rose from the lake holding Excalibur, the sword of King Arthur of Britain. She was foster mother to Lancelot, best-loved of the Knights of the Round Table. To rid herself of the pestering love of the **Wizard,** Merlin, she sealed him up in a rock. Not, however, without first learning all his magic. She, herself, will never die. Pale as moonshine on deep water, she will always be the mysterious Lady of the Lake.

Lamassu are the lovely Assyrian **Guardian Angels** without whom life would be torment. Neither quite gods nor quite human, they are winged bulls with the heads of men. They carry people's prayers to the gods and bring back divine favors from above.

Lamed Vuv are thirty-six holy Jewish men. Because of their righteousness, the whole world is allowed to survive—in spite of its corruption. Humble men, unrecognized as saints, they only come forward if tragedy threatens, to guide their people to safety. Then, unknown and unthanked, they disappear again.

Lamia was a wretched queen of Libya whose children were all killed in a fit of jealousy by the Greek goddess Hera. Crazed by her grief, Lamia became a monster with a woman's head and a snake's body. She roamed the countryside sucking the life out of any child she could grab. Later, she multiplied until there were hundreds of Lamias relentlessly searching for children to eat. As their numbers grew, these monsters slowly developed a new shape. They became part sharp-clawed bear and part nimble goat, while their bodies glistened all over with moist, fishy scales. Their faces remained human and all resembled their ancestress—the sad, obsessive, Queen of Libya.

Lares and Penates were Roman household gods, whose images, roughly whittled out of wood, stood near the hearth. Every day the father of the family offered them small food sacrifices and asked them for help in his family affairs. Lares usually represented the spirits of the family's founding ancestor.

Larvae and Lemures are the ghosts of wicked dead men. Each May at the feast day of the dead, these sinister ghouls rise from their dank graves to haunt the living. Then the father of every Roman family, standing with his back to the Larvae, throws black beans over his shoulder to drive them away. The specters, who detest beans, are compelled to pick them up and slink back into the earth until the next May.

Leontophontes are smallish creatures that could be animals or plants, depending on how you look at them. Their flesh is deadly poison to lions so hunters use them as lion bait. For this reason, the King of Beasts detests little Leontophontes and will squash them with his paws if he ever gets the chance.

Leprechauns, or Little People, are the small Irish fairies. Fair-haired and child-sized, you may see them out of the corner of your eye—dressed in red and green, dancing on a moonlit night. Although they are clever at trickery and illusion, they never tell lies or give away a secret.

Leshy is a Slavic woodland spirit, Guardian of the Forest. His eyes are bulgy, his face blue, his long beard green, and he wears his clothes all backward and inside out.

Leviathan is the brilliant, primordial fish or water serpent who lives in the Mediterranean Sea. Longer than twenty winding rivers placed end to end, this monstrous **Snake** of dazzling eyes and luminous, shiny scales was created by God on the fifth day of time. God also gave him a female but soon destroyed her, fearing that, should she multiply, there would be no more space in the world.

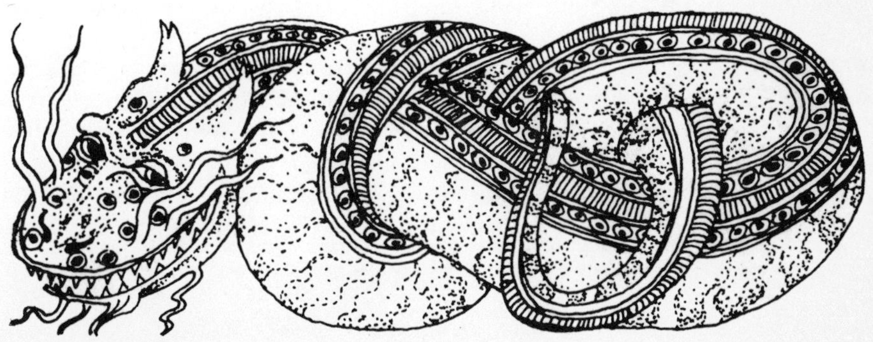

Lilith is the stately and silent demon woman given to be Adam's first wife. She was unable to bear children, so God created the fair and fruitful Eve whom Adam loved and took to wife. Cold Lilith was cast out and, in revenge, steals children at night, pretending they are her own.

Lion is the prancing King of Beasts. Frolicsome and happy, he is also proud, courageous, and wary, never closing his eyes even in sleep. If his mane is curly, he is peaceful, but, if it is straight, he is of an angry disposition. The Winged Lion, symbol of Saint Mark, is very wise in the use of medicines. It is rumored that when the lion is himself ill, eating a monkey will soon cure him. Lions, however, eat very little and only when hungry.

Loch Ness Monster is an enormous **Sea Serpent** who has been trapped for hundreds of years in a Scottish lake.

Lorelei, a lovely, elusive nymph, is a daughter of the Rhine. She sits on treacherous rocks in the swirling river, toying with a comb as gold as her hair. Her eyes roam across the water, and she sings songs of such sad sweetness that no man can resist her. And so men come—rich and poor alike—only to be sucked down into the wild currents at her feet.

Lotophagi are a peaceful people who live not so very far away. By eating lotus blossoms, they maintain a floating, dream-filled state of lethargy. Neither care nor worry dims their heavy-lidded eyes. The Greek hero, Odysseus, came across them in his travels but hurried away, in case, tempted to eat the exquisite lotus blossom, he should forget his wife and country and remain forever in the hallucinatory land of the Lotus Eaters.

Lucifer, God's brilliant "Light Bearer," was a mighty prince among **Angels.** But his pride grew too great and he was hurled from Heaven into the darkness below. As he fell, the blue sapphire from his crown tumbled to earth where, many eons later, it was shaped into the Holy Grail, now guarded by the mysterious **Fisher King.** And Lucifer, Prince of **Devils,** walks the earth like a great dark shadow, trying to redeem his lost glory by enticing human disciples.

Lung is the Chinese **Dragon** who travels around the world on mysterious magnetic paths, along which birds also migrate. The Lung control wind, rain, and hidden treasures, while one even guards the flaming Sun Pearl. There are also five Sea Dragon Kings who cause terrible typhoons on their yearly flight to report to the Emperor of Heaven.

Mab is a tiny English **Fairy** Queen. Her chariot is a burnished hazelnut shell drawn by flying ants. As she drives magically down airy currents, her cape, a single, precious orchid petal, flutters about her minute shoulders. It is said she carries dreams, carefully folded on the seat beside her to give to those who sleep only lightly.

Maenads were Greek women, devotees of Dionysus, god of the vine and of the senses. Maddened by narcotics and wine, the priestesses danced wildly across the countryside, celebrating their orgiastic rites. If anyone were foolish enough to stand in their way, he was mercilessly dismembered and scattered in small pieces, as was the **Muse**'s son, sad Orpheus. The **Satyrs** and **Sileni** often joined in these raucous festivities.

Magicians are learned men of great, even superhuman, powers. While masters of magic and teachers of witchcraft, they are not as influential in other worlds as are the **Wizards** The greatest teachers of magic are two **Angels** named Harut and Marut. These two are presently being punished for past sins by being hung from their feet in a deep, dark cavern near Babel. Men wishing to become magicians go to them at dead of night to learn the secrets of the gods.

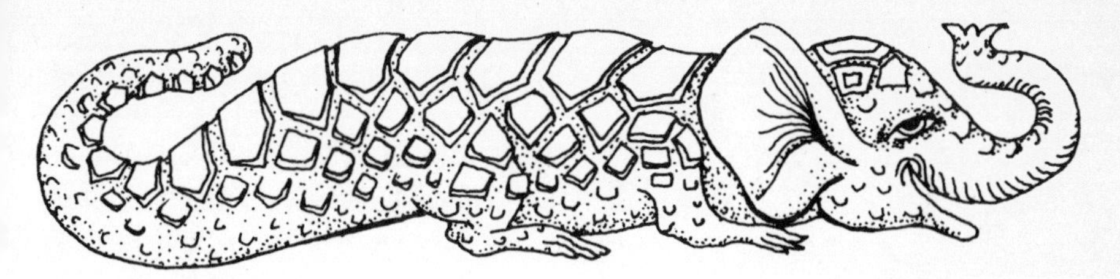

Makara, steed of the Indian **Moon** and water god, Varuna, is a wondrously versatile creature. Partly wise elephant, partly cruel crocodile, or, as some say, part deer, part fish, he is both aquatic and terrestrial. He can also fly through the sky to carry the pale moon god each night; or swim the wide oceans, regulating tides; or walk across the dry earth while his master distributes rewards and punishments among men.

Manatee is the large and ungainly grandmother of **Mermaids.** This peaceable sea cow clasps her babes gently to her breast as she rocks among the waves. Delighted by music, she sways and dances lumberingly whenever she hears it.

Mandrake, the deadly Mandragora, is a plant whose root is a perfectly formed manikin, or little man. It grows at the foot of a recently occupied gallows tree. When it is plucked, it screams so terribly that all who hear it either go mad or die. But once a man owns one, and if he wraps it in silk and treats it well, he will be very fortunate. Both the male Mandrake, which is white, and the red or black female have great secret, magical powers.

Mannanan Mac-Lir is the three-legged son of a Celtic woman and a god. He is a solar and fertility god who, whirling across the sky on his three legs, represents the solar house of morning, noon, and evening as well as the seasonal times of planting, growth, and harvest. He is the deity of the death and rebirth of all things, and, as such, is ruler of the Island of Eternal Youth that lies in the sea to the west of Ireland.

Manticora is the lion-man of the Indies whose cries shrill between his triple row of pointed teeth. His eyes burn blue as fire, and deadly quills shoot from his tail while he stalks his favorite food: Man.

Mara, the Indian **Devil,** came riding on storm clouds to destroy Lord Buddha as he meditated. But his weapon turned to flowers in the air.

Maruts, in Indian mythology, are the forty-nine gigantic sons of Death and Winter. They are tempestuous weather gods who herd the lightning-charged clouds across the sky. As their feet pound thunderously over the mountain tops, the earth trembles for miles around with the fearful expectancy that precedes the wild storms of the cold season.

Medusa was the youngest and only mortal of the three snaky-haired Gorgons. They have brazen hands and saliva glistens on their long sharp tusks. One look from their probing eyes turns men to stone, and when the Greek hero, Perseus, cut off Medusa's head, all the snakes of Africa oozed from her bloody eye. Perseus, made invisible by his helmet, managed to kill the monster with a bronze sickle while watching her indirectly through his mirrored shield.

Melpomene is the sadly soulful **Muse** of tragedy.

Melusina is a golden-haired, watery-eyed, French fairy girl. During the Middle Ages, she married a mortal, the noble Raymond of Lusignan. She made the condition that he should never see her on Saturday. But curious, one Saturday, he spied on her and saw that on that day she was a mermaid. When Melusina discovered that he knew her secret, she flew away, promising to return only at each new lord's birth.

Memnon, handsome king of Ethiopia, was the son of Eos, rosy-cheeked Greek goddess of dawn. When he was killed, a colossal statue was erected to commemorate him. But his loving mother has never forgotten her beautiful warrior son, and, each morning as the sun's first rays fall on the stone figure, a sad lament comes from it. Legends say this strange cry is the eternal weeping of the dawn, mourning her lost son, while all around the world the drops of dew that sparkle at first light are her bittersweet tears shed daily in his memory.

Mermaids are half-maid, half-fish, and as fair to look on as a wind-tossed summer sea. Combing their green-gold hair or leaping playfully through the waves, they flash their silvery fishy tails in the sun. Musical and charming, they sing sad songs of longing for a soul they never had. To see them swim gaily at the prow of a ship warns of stormy seas and inclement weather. Some mermaids marry mortal men and become as kind and faithful as a human wife. But there may come a day when the call of the ocean is too strong to resist and the wife goes back to her watery home.

Mermecolion, the Ant-lion, is the rare offspring of an ant and a lion. This obstinate creature is not long-lived, for its ant half refuses meat and its lion half will not eat grains. Thus, starving itself, it soon dies. The old books compare Mermecolion to the man who fails because he is unable to make decisions.

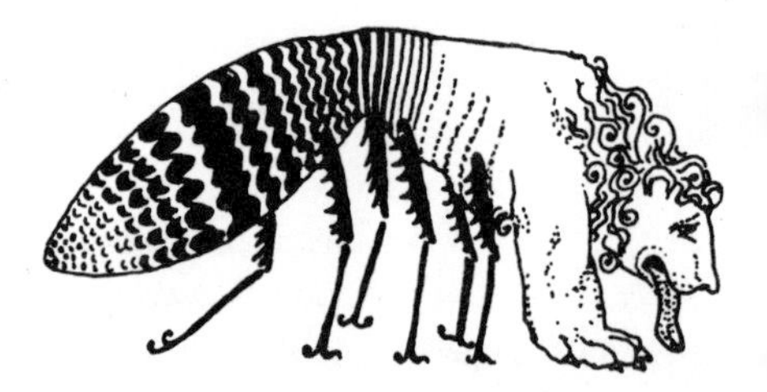

Merrows are water people who live on dry land under the sea near Ireland. The men are extraordinarily ugly: their hair and teeth are mossy green, their noses large and red; they are covered with scales, and their short, stumpy arms resemble the fins of a fat fish. Altogether unlike their mates, the females are both pretty and charming. All the Merrows wear little red caps, in which lies their power to cross down unharmed to their palaces below water. If a mortal man can steal the red cap of a Merrow girl, he may take her to wife.

Mimir, the one who knows, was a **Jotun** who guarded the well of wisdom. Odin, lord of the Teutonic gods, paid with one of his eyes for a drink of that water. When Mimir died, Odin had his head embalmed and asked its advice in emergencies.

Minotaur—half man, half bull—was a heinous flesh-eating monster. He was the son of Pasiphae, queen of Crete, who, hidden in a mechanical bronze cow, mated with a white bull. He lived in an intricate palace, called the Labyrinth, from which no man could escape. Yearly, he was fed a tribute of seven maids and seven men until he was killed by the Greek hero, Theseus.

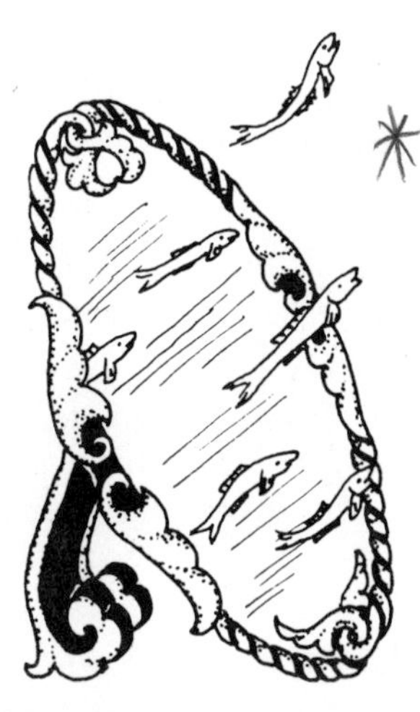

✳ **Mirror People** used to walk the world freely, but they rebelled and were locked within their mirrors by the Yellow Emperor of China. One day, a silvery line will quiver across the glass. This will be the Mirror Fish, first to shimmer from his prison, leading all the other reflected creatures to freedom. Wave on wave, their forces will grow as every mirror yields its captives. Soon, joined by the water people, their ranks will conquer the world.

Moerae are the Greek **Fates,** stern daughters of Themis, goddess of law.

Molionids were twin sons of the Greek sea god Poseidon. They were hatched together from a single silver egg. Many people believe that they shared the same body because they resembled each other so much both in mind and looks, although they had separate heads, arms, and legs. While in the service of King Augeias, they were both slain by mighty Hercules.

Moloch is a fiery and bloodthirsty idol with a vast furnace burning in his belly. He has great power and an insatiable appetite, especially for children. When the Kingdom of Israel was in danger, all the young wives, seeking his favor and protection, took their own babies to be fed to him as sacrifices. This gory tradition probably came from the neighboring country of Babylonia which was renowned for its many **Necromancers.**

Monkey was a restless and inquisitive creature who set out to conquer the universe. To quiet him, the gods put him in charge of the Peaches of Immortality. He simply ate all the peaches, becoming immortal himself. For this supreme impudence, he was imprisoned in a mountain. Finally, a merciful goddess decided that if he traveled to the Western Paradise and brought Buddha's teachings back to China, his past would be forgiven.

Monopods are a unique race whom the great explorer, Mandeville, met while traveling in Africa. As their name implies, they each have only one foot. As it gets tiresome to hop along on one foot, it is their custom, during the heat of the day, to lie on their backs with their leg extended above them. In this position, their large, flat feet act as umbrellas to shade them from the burning Ethiopian sun.

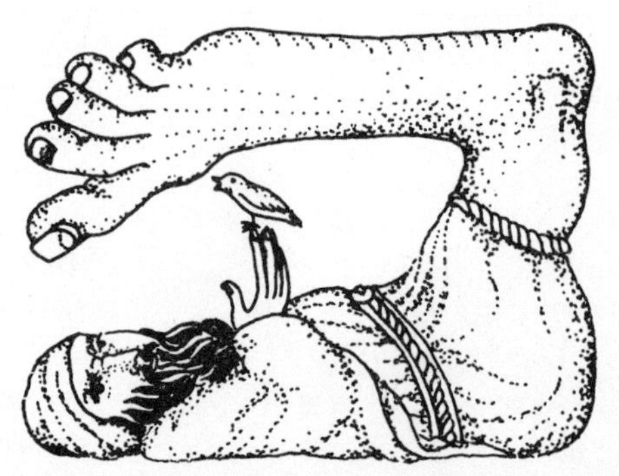

Moon, bright eye of night, has long been populated by all sorts of spirits and strange lovely creatures. The Japanese speak of a hare sitting in the moon, happily eating rice cakes, while Americans say the moon swallowed a frog whose pale outline can be distinguished in its center.

The Chinese speak of the CELESTIAL TOAD; Once there was a woman graceful and lovely as golden bamboo. Her name was Heng-O, and she was married to an archer so skillful that the gods had rewarded him with an elixir that would enable him to live forever. One day, while he was away, Heng-O tasted the elixir of immortality. It was so delicious that she drank it down to the very last drop. Suddenly, it occurred to her that her husband would be very angry; so, she ran to the moon to hide. There she lives now, disguised as a delicate gold toad, controlling the world's life-giving waters.

The first MAN IN THE MOON was Sin, the Sumerian god of astrology and divination. This mysterious blue-bearded shaman nightly sails his crescent moon-boat across the oceans of the sky.

SISTER SUN AND BROTHER MOON appear in American Indian and Eskimo stories: Long ago, a radiantly beautiful woman was visited secretly every evening by a lover. He always came after dark and she had never seen his face. Longing to know who he was, one night she slyly marked him with ashes. The next day she saw that the ashes marked her own brother. In horror, she fled into the sky where she became the splendid shining sun. Her brother ran after her and still follows her around the sky as the wan moon mottled with ashy stains.

VARUNA, the stern moon god of India, rides through the skies on his strange steed, the **Makara.** With stars in his eyes and the wind in his mouth, a thousand white horses prance about him as he maneuvers the flow of the tides and the lash of the rain. He rules the dead, whose home is the moon, and guards the sacred nectar, Soma, that is kept there to nourish the gods. No thought or action in the universe, however secret, can be hidden from his all-seeing, all-knowing eyes.

In Greece, there are three Moon Goddesses: the virgin huntress **ARTEMIS,** is the young crescent. Inaccessible and pure, she protects newborn babies. The full, Mother Moon, is **SELENE.** She fell in love with Endymion, a youth who was granted eternal life and beauty as long as he remains asleep. Every night, she caresses his sleeping eyes with her silvery light, and fifty watery daughters have been born to them. The third Greek Moon is **HECATE,** broad-winged goddess of the dark side of the moon. Greatest of all witches, she flies—invisible—through wild night winds, surrounded by her pack of spectral hounds.

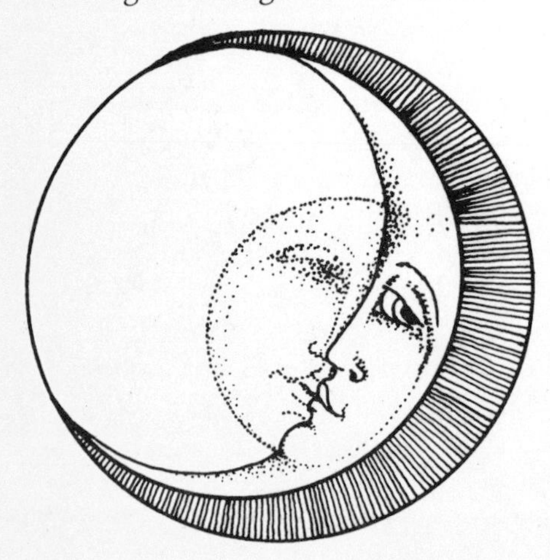

LUNA was the medieval **Alchemists'** name for the lovely lady moon. She is the White Queen or Goddess who represents the silvery part of their Great Work of Transmutation. Some say the moon is a man as it waxes to fullness and a woman as it wanes. Moon stories are endless, but all agree that her mystery is great and her changes powerful.

Mooncalf is the illegitimate child of a **Witch** and her **Incubus** dream lover.

Morgana La Fé (from "fee", French word for "fairy") is an evil **Sorceress,** sister of King Arthur of Britain. She lives eternally on the isle of Avalon with her enchanted lover, Ogier the Dane.

Muses are the nine daughters of Zeus and Mnemosyne, memory. They were created to sing the eternal praise of the Greek Gods who triumphed over the **Titans.** Wrapped in night's shadows, they secretly visit the sleeping world, distributing songs of inspiration and prophecy.

CALLIOPE, eloquent Muse of Epic Poetry, became the mother of sad Orpheus, greatest musician of all.

EUTERPE is the flute-playing Muse of Music.

CLIO, Muse of History, sounds the victory trumpet. She fell madly in love with the King of Macedonia, whose nine daughters were turned into magpies for presuming to be more poetic than the Muses.

THALIA, Muse of Comedy, was also associated with pastoral scenes and even fertility rites. She is said to be mother of the CORYBANTES, furious priests of the Corn Goddess, Cybele.

MELPOMENE, Muse of Tragedy, gave birth to the silver-voiced **Sirens.** These beguiling daughters, flaunting their talents challenged the Muses to a singing contest. They lost and, in punishment, their wings were snipped from their shoulders.

TERPSICHORE is the graceful Muse of Dance and Lyric Poetry.

POLYHYMNIA, Muse of Sacred Song and Dance also inspires the silent art of Mime.

URANIA is the Muse of Astronomy. She plucks the chord in men that vibrates to the rhythm of stars, enabling them to hear the Celestial Harmony.

Muryans are the Cornish **Pixies.** Because of some forgotten misdeed, these fairy people have been condemned to dwindle away, becoming smaller and smaller, until they will soon be invisible.

Myrmidons were a swarm of ants whom Zeus, Father of Greek Gods, turned into men to repopulate the island of Aegina which had been devastated by plagues. Like many soldiers today, these Ant-men were often called to fight in wars because of their blind obedience to orders. Determined and dimwitted as ants, they carried out even the most savage commands, never once stopping to doubt or question their leaders' motives.

Nagas and their wives, the Naginis, are the semidivine snake people of India. Although they have the power to assume other shapes, they usually appear as half-human, half-snake, or in their wholly snaky bodies. Sometimes, a Naga has three or even seven cobra heads spreading out like a jeweled fan above his single coiled body. Because of their wily ingenuity, the Nagas are often sent by the gods to carry out their divine laws.

Naiads are the Greek fresh-water **Nymphs.** Their hair is hung with sparkling drops and their laughter echoes on the softly gurgling stream. The Naiads are as elusive as the rushing springs they live in. Yet, if prayed to, their waters can cure any illness. One drink from their brooks will produce strange visions of the future and inspire poetry in the souls of those that seek their help.

Nasatyas, or Aswins, are handsome Indian twins, young Heralds of the Dawn. The chill of night melts in the warmth of their bright eyes and golden skin. They fly up over the cool horizon in a dazzling, three-wheeled chariot drawn by countless flocks of birds. Wise physicians, these sunny twins restore youth and vitality to both gods and men.

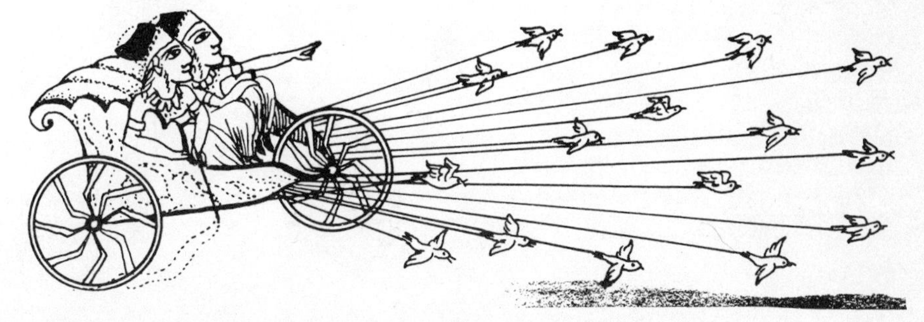

Nasnas is a half-man with a woeful human voice who prowls the lonely deserts of Arabia. Child of a desert demon and a mortal, this deficient creature is born with only half a body, and, or so it is said, it is twice as hard for him to love as he has only half a heart.

Necromancers are evil **Magicians.** Trading in black magic and weaving dark spells, many acquire both riches and power. They have no regard for anyone else as they relentlessly pursue their selfish goals, and, sooner or later, their evil comes back at them in unforeseen and horrible ways.

Nemesis, sister of the **Fates,** is Divine Anger. No immorality escapes her dark, piercing eyes and inevitable punishment. Jealous of any man too rich or too happy, she angrily turns the wheel of justice until he pays in sorrows for his former glory. So speak softly of your luck and share your wealth in case, becoming too fortunate, you excite the jealousy of the angry Greek goddess.

Nereids are the fifty **Nymph** daughters of the Sea.

Nethelim were fiery and aerial giants. In the earth's early days, some of God's angels looked down from Heaven and saw the great beauty of mortal women. Because they were tempted to love the daughters of man, God cast them out of Heaven. These outcast angels fell to earth where they mated with women and whispered to them the secrets of the gods. The children of these unnatural marriages were the first magicians, the red-eyed, white, woolly-haired Nethelim.

Nia are African nature spirits who can be helpful or harmful according to their mood. To pacify them before starting a journey, the wise man makes them offerings: leaves to calm the Airy Nia, a ball of red mud for the Earth Nia, flowers to please the River Nia. And if the Nia of the Forest are to help, a virgin must bury a white egg under a sacred tree.

Nibelungs are the Teutonic **Dwarves** who, led by **Alberich,** guarded the fabled treasure of King Nibelung, which was later lost in the Rhine.

Nightmares are brought by the Old English demon goddess, Mara. She comes softly in the night to steal away children or touches sleeping eyes with her icy fingers while terrible visions fill the air. It is said that a potion prepared from dried dragon eyes and honey will keep this horrid demon away. If the dragon eyes are not available, a simple teaspoonful of honey at bedtime will ensure a sweet, dream-filled sleep.

Nineve is the mysterious and watery **Lady Of The Lake.**

Nisse is the Danish **Brownie** who, if appreciated, brings good fortune.

Nixies, the German water **Nymphs,** seem too beautiful to be so cruel. They sit by the riverbank combing their golden hair while their melancholy voices murmur strange, lovely songs. Any man who hears one is driven mad with desire for her. But if he has the audacity to take her in his arms, she lures him to a watery death beneath the waves.

Norns are the Teutonic **Fates.** At first, there were many of these weird women. They came to crowd around each newborn child; the good ones showered blessings while the evil ones muttered curses. Later, the Norns dwindled to three: Urd, the eldest, looks to the past, Verdandi to the present, and Skuld, with veiled eyes, foreshadows the future. Sitting for all time by the roots of the great world tree, they spin out the fragile threads of life.

Nuckelavee is a slimy, skinless monster who terrifies Scottish fishing villages. Rising dripping from the cold gray sea, he looks like a horse and rider long since melted together into one grotesque formless form. On misty days, his rotting stench and stinking breath spreads pestilence and death along the shoreline.

Nymphs are the lovely, protective nature spirits. Their girlish forms hide shyly in trees, meadows, and water, and they are named accordingly: **Nereids** of salt water; **Naiads** of fresh; **Dryads** and **Hamadryads** in trees; and **Oreads** in mountain caves. Though naturally gentle, if they feel threatened, they attack with magic spells and frightful curses. Many have spoken of men punished with death for surprising a nymph or goddess naked, for their beauty is too wondrous for mortal eyes and their love too heavy for a mortal heart to bear. Although nymphs do not age, after ten thousand years, they die and disappear completely. Like the fairies, they have no souls.

Oannes is an ancient Babylonian water god who lives in the Persian Gulf. Both man and fish, he spreads his wisdom throughout both his underwater kingdom and on the coast. He taught men civilization: how to cultivate the soil with plants and the mind with understanding. He is also master of unearthly wisdom and prophesy.

Oberon, glamorous King of the **Fairies,** derived his name from the Teutonic Elf of Dwarf King, **Alberich,** guardian of untold earthly treasures.

Oceanids are the three thousand **Nymph** daughters of Oceanus, whose unending waters encircle the universe. Flirting in frothy waves of cosmic seas, they receive the stars each night into their rippling arms.

Og was the only giant to survive the devastating Biblical flood. He promised to be Noah's slave, so the patriarch allowed him to perch his immense body on the roof of the Ark, and fed him through a hole in the side. He was killed five hundred years later when he tried to attack Moses.

*****Ogres** are stormy and destructive **Giants** who haunt wild mountains and lonely bogs. Even less intelligent than Giants, Ogres seldom think of anything besides eating. All day, they hunt their wasteland habitat for succulent human beings foolish enough to pass that way. At night all the Ogre families gather around enormous campfires, their pointy teeth watering in anticipation, while they roast the traveler who is to be their dinner.

Oni, of Japan, are huge, horned devil-giants. Their skin is bilious green or red, and traces of their huge footprints can be found on remote mountainsides. It is the Oni's job to load sinners into their fiery chariots and drive them off to Hell. They also spread deathly diseases and plagues, but are actually not as hard-hearted as they may seem. If they are shown respect and kindness, they can become quite friendly and helpful.

Ooser, the Dorset **Devil,** is probably the last demon left walking the earth in his physical shape. He cavorts through the English village streets dressed in tattered cowskins with a skillful pair of vicious pincers with which he torments and frightens children. He has long horns, shaggy hair, and rolling, protruding eyes. His stiff, grim jaw is frozen in a mocking leer at the terrified shrieks of his victims.

Ophion, the cosmic snake, was son of the first Greek Goddess of All. After he was born, his mother laid an egg around which Ophion wrapped his body, coil on coil, to keep it warm. When the time came, the egg burst open and all the universe fell out. Then the goddess, angered at Ophion's proud boast that it was he who had created the world, threw him from Heaven in disgrace. Ophites are a religious sect who worship **Snakes** as a symbol of wisdom.

Orc was a monster fish of such greed that at one meal he could eat up all the creatures of the universe. He may be related to his predecessor, the early Roman god of death, Orcus, for death certainly devours all things at one time or another.

Oreads are the lovely, leafy **Nymphs** of lonely mountains and secret grottoes. Usually kind-hearted, these shy, girlish spirits can, however, fly into a rage if a messy or noisy traveler desecrates their places and upsets the peace.

Orion, the beautiful and passionate Greek hunter, was a giant who could walk on earth or water. Once, his eyes were angrily picked out by the father of a girl he eloped with. Striding out over the eastern sea, the rays of the rising sun restored his sight. Athene, Goddess of Wisdom, loved him, but shot him with her arrow by mistake. Anguished at his death, she placed him among the stars, together with his faithful dog, Sirius.

Orthros was a terrible dog with bristling fur and two fearful, grimacing heads. He guarded a bloodthirsty herd of flesh-eating red oxen that belonged to the ugly monster **Geryon.** Finally, this unnatural animal and his master were killed by the Greek hero, Hercules, who came to steal away the cattle as one of his Twelve Labors.

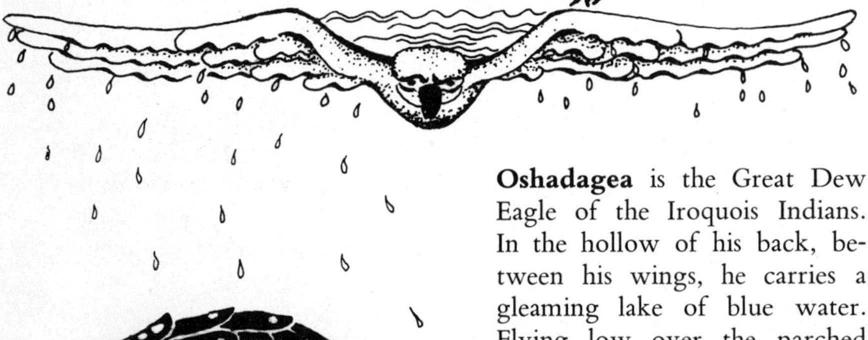

Oshadagea is the Great Dew Eagle of the Iroquois Indians. In the hollow of his back, between his wings, he carries a gleaming lake of blue water. Flying low over the parched earth, he dips his feather tips into this heavenly lake and sprinkles the land with dew. Then, leaving the world refreshed, the Great Eagle flies back into the sunset where he lives in the western sky.

Ouroboros, the **Snake** who devours his own tail, is the **Alchemists'** symbol of life, an unending cycle of energy. Such a serpent also surrounds the world, separating the order within its sphere from the chaos that struggles beyond.

Poltergeists are invisible but very active energy forces. Sometimes brazenly impudent, they storm through a room and, before your very eyes, start hurling every movable object helter-skelter with speedy unseen hands.

Pooka is a horrible, red-eyed, shaggy colt that roams the wilds of Ireland. Rattling his chains, he scares wayfarers half out of their wits. In England, he became Puck, the mischievous but lovable fairy boy who often takes on the shape of a colt.

Poppets, in medieval England, were small dolls made by **Witches** in the image of a particularly disliked person. When a witch wanted to give her enemy a headache, she chanted a painful spell while insidiously jabbing a pin into the Poppet's head. At the same moment, however many miles away he was, the man she cursed felt it. And if she drove a needle into the doll's heart, she might even cause a man to die. Poppets could be made of any material, but, usually, they were either wax or stuffed rag dolls.

Poreskoro, among the Transylvanian Gypsies, is the last and most terrible son of the beautiful fairy queen and her horrible demon husband. He has four cat heads, four dog heads, and a poisonous viper tail. Slinking among the Gypsy caravans, he spreads plague, cholera, and other devastating epidemics.

Prester John was the mysterious medieval Christian king of the Indies. Little is known of him except from a letter he sent to the Pope. In it he described some of the marvels of his vast domain, which extended from Burma in the East to Ethiopia in the West. He spoke of unicorns and centaurs, of dragon tamers, and other magical people; and, above, all, he described his untold wealth and power.

Pretas are rather vague **Ghosts** who loiter menacingly in Indian graveyards.

Prometheus was the **Titan** who mingled his tears with earth to create the first man. When he brought fire as a gift to earth, the angry Greek gods chained him to a rock as punishment.

Puck is one of the names of the helpful sprite usually called **Robin Goodfellow** in England. Among his favorite disguises is that of a shaggy colt like the Celtic **Pooka.**

Punch and his wife, Judy, are traditional characters of English puppetry. He is a comically grotesque hunchback with a great hooked nose and painted chin, who quarrels constantly and even clubs to death everyone who opposes him. Punch, derived from the Italian Punchinello, is, in reality a vulgar and humorous form of the Devil. Nevertheless, Punch usually outwits the Devil when they meet.

Purusha is the Indian **Giant** Lord of the Universe, who sprang from a golden egg floating on cosmic waters. He was lonely; so, dividing himself in half, he gave birth to all the universe to keep him company.

Quat is the creator god of Oceania. In the beginning of the world, people complained bitterly that having daylight all the time was boring. So Quat set out on an expedition to buy some nighttime from Night who lived in a distant country. Soon he returned to his island people, bringing with him both the night and the dawn which he also bought—in exchange for a large pig. He carefully taught his people how to sleep and also provided roosters and other birds to wake them up when it was time for daylight to be uncovered again every morning.

Queen of Sheba, Bilkis by name, was a wise and powerful woman. However, rumor had spread to neighboring lands that she had, instead of feet, the hooves of a goat. To test this strange tale, King Solomon, noted for his wisdom, had his palace floors paved with glass and invited the great queen to visit. When she arrived, thinking that the shiny surface was water, she daintily lifted up her skirt so as not to wet it as she crossed the floor. All present were relieved to see that she had as human and as pretty a pair of feet as any woman.

Quetzalcoatl, the Plumed Snake god of the early Mexican Indians, was a red-haired white man who came out of the sea to lead the people and teach them the arts of civilization. Then, one day, when he had stayed long enough, promising that he would return when the time was right, he flew off into the sky where he became the Morning Star, Venus.

Ra is the falcon-headed Egyptian **Sun** god. Lord of the Universe, he fathered the gods, while Man and all other living things sprang from his tears. At night, he is a baby, safely sleeping in the lotus bud afloat on dark waters waiting to be reborn each morning. During the day, as he travels through the twelve Hourly Sky Kingdoms, he grows older. When evening comes, he falls back into the dark, a tired and decrepit old man.

Rainbow Snake is an earth god. Reaching into the sky to drink, he becomes a shimmering, many-colored bridge between heaven and earth for gods and angels to walk back and forth across.

Rakshasas are terrible Indian demons who molest and torture human beings. Like their king, **Ravana,** they can assume any shape they choose, being artful magicians, but, at home, they are deformed, troll-like creatures with twisted limbs and misshapen faces.

Ravana was the blood-thirsty king of Rakshasas. Each of his twenty demonic heads was armed with fangs sharp as crescent moons, while his mountainous body literally bristled with arms. He was at last overcome by Rama, god-hero of the epic poem, "Ramayana."

Ravens called Thought and Memory acted as messengers between the early Teutonic races and their gods. In later times, ravens were called harbingers of death.

Remora is the small and pesky hindrance fish. It swims in large schools that attach themselves to the bottom of ships for a free ride. Consequently, they slow down the boat's progress and annoy all concerned. Some say they have feet, others say wings, but the point is, they are a nuisance except when used as a love charm; even then, they don't always work.

Rishis are the holiest and wisest men of India. The seven first and greatest of the Rishis, whose spiritual excellence knows no bounds, can be seen shining as stars in the constellation that we call the Great Bear. These seven sages are so holy that their power sometimes exceeds that of the gods themselves. Even their bones have hidden magical properties, and of these, the storm god, Indra, made his deadly, flashing thunderbolt. These wise and learned men are the ancestors of all priests and teachers in India.

Robin Goodfellow is the magical son of a mortal girl and a fairy man. Carefree and laughter loving, he often helps around the house, as do the **Brownies,** or plays mad pranks on the country folk. He is amorous and beautiful and can change his shape at will. Later, he became the well-known Robin Hood of English ballads who lived in the greenwood and stole from the rich to give to the poor.

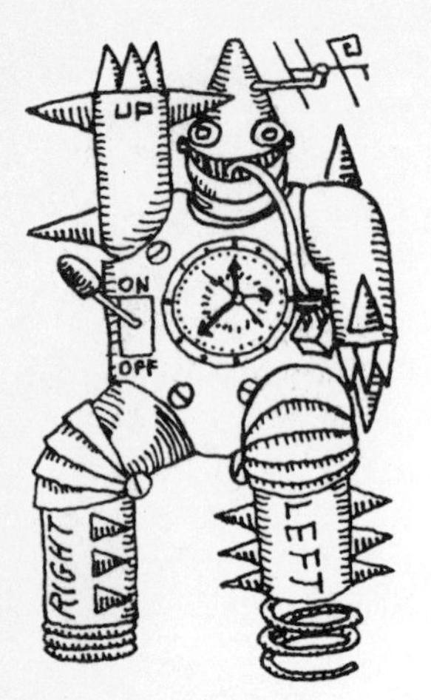

Robots are humanoid figures created by skillful and magical men. They move and may even speak as do living creatures but, having no soul, they are not truly alive. Palaces have been built and wars waged by robots at the command of their makers, who may even consult them as oracles in times of uncertainty. Great care must be taken to control these mechanical men because it has often happened that the robots rise up against their masters to destroy them. Whether these mishaps occur by accident or intent is not known.

Rukh, or Roc, is an enormous bird living in the South Indian Ocean Islands. It is like an eagle, but of a marvelously great size. Its wings are so strong and their span so wide that a man may ride beneath them without the bird noticing. It has even been seen easily seizing an elephant in its talons and flying away with it.

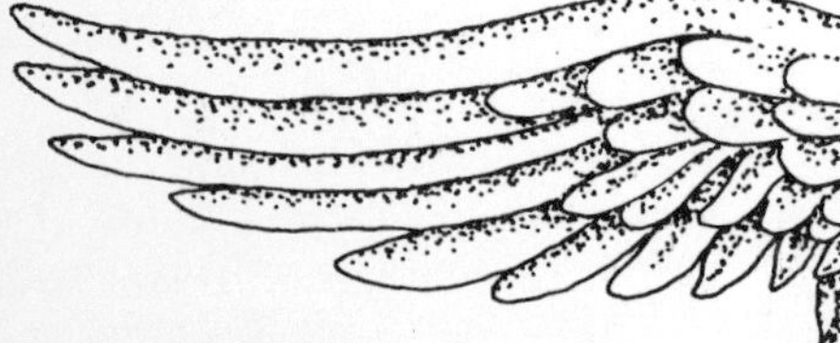

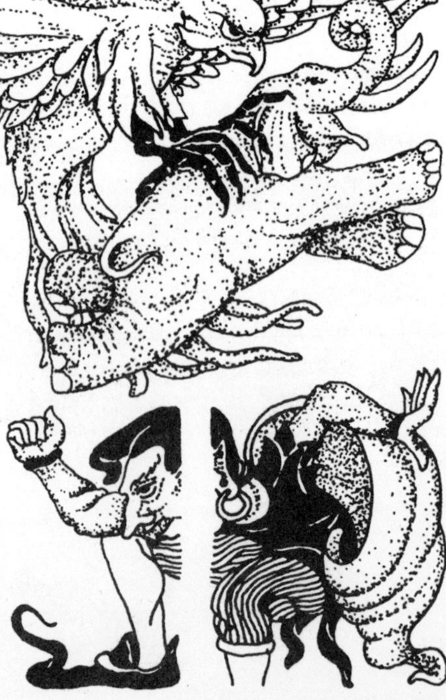

Rumpelstiltskin is a peevish little German **Dwarf.** Once he helped a princess get out of her prison tower on condition that she give him her first-born son. The girl agreed, but when her son was born she begged the Dwarf not to take it. Quite sure of his secret, he gave her three days to guess his name or he would certainly take the child. Just in time, the princess, discovering his name, said "Rumpelstiltskin!" Whereupon, the little man flew into a rage, and stamping his foot right into the floor, split in half.

Sack-Man is the Spanish "Hombre del Saco." A sinister, shabby old man, he slinks down dark, cobbled streets on misty days looking for children who have gotten lost in the maze of back alleys. On his back, he carries a large sack bulging with mysterious, squirming bumps. These bumps are all the children who have been unfortunate enough to meet up with him and have been popped into his bag. The ones he carries away are never seen again.

*** Salamanders** are the lizardlike rulers of the element Fire. They are rarely seen. When the young Italian, Benvenuto Cellini, saw one, his father thorougly boxed his ears so that he should never forget. These little dragons dart about unharmed in the flames and their skin is so cold that they actually put out the fire around them. **Prester John,** the legendary king, had a cloak made of a thousand fireproof Salamander skins.

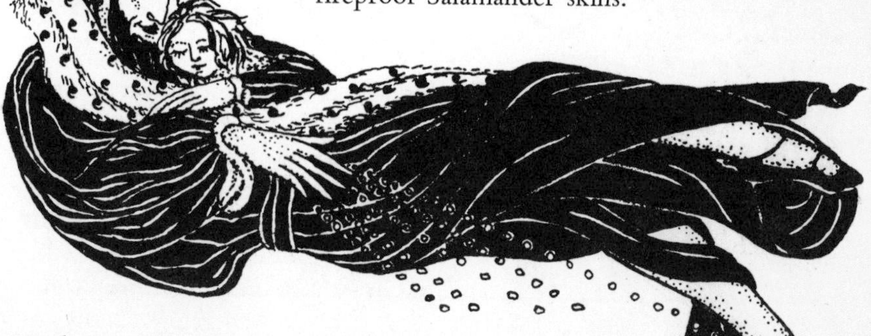

Sandman comes flying, wrapped in night to sprinkle golden sleep-dust in children's eyes. Those who have been particularly good and are not afraid of the dark, he will fold in his starry cloak and carry through marvelous dreamlands until the morning.

Santa Claus is the jolly old Father of Christmas. Bundled in furs, he leaps from his sleigh, and, sliding down chimneys, leaves lovely surprises in children's stockings. He derives his name from venerable Saint Nicholas, who, one day many years ago, entered a dark tavern by the roadside. In the basement, he discovered three children who had been pickled in a barrel of brine by the wicked inkeeper and his wife. Saint Nick pulled the unfortunate babes from their grisly tub and promptly restored them to life. Since then, he has been the patron saint of children, his name passed on and made famous by the much-loved Santa.

Sara-Mama is the fruitful, life-giving Corn Mother. She comes to earth in the form of strangely shaped or especially large ears of corn which the Peruvians adorn with rich clothes and worship to ensure a plentiful harvest.

Satan is the name given to the angel, **Lucifer,** after his fall from Heaven.

Satyrs are rude, lewd creatures with human torso and bandy, hairy, goat legs, goat horns, and inquisitive pointed ears. They are older and more fully grown than their naughty Roman cousins, the **Fauns.** Whistling wildly joyful music on reed pipes, they scare the gentle woodland Nymphs. As companions to the wine god, Dionysus, during his drunken festivals, the Satyrs dance and play ecstatically with the crazed **Maenad** priestesses.

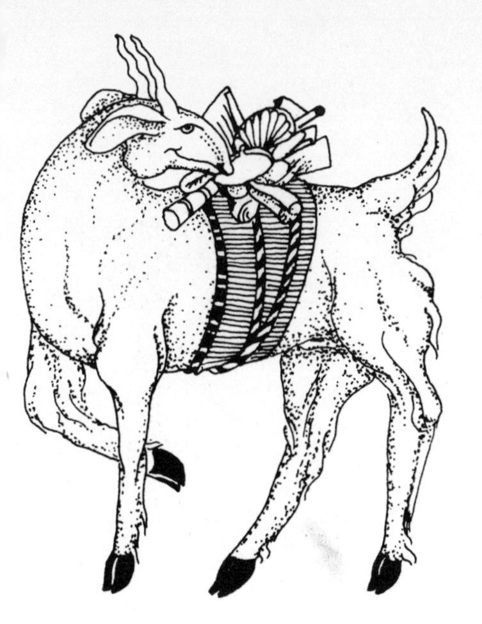

Scapegoat was a goat into which the Jewish high priest symbolically deposited all the ills and evils of his people on the Day of Atonement. The goat was then driven beyond the city walls and either stoned to death or sent away into the wilderness never to be seen again. In this way, the people, cleansed and rid of all their sins, were ready to start a new year free of guilt. Among other races, various animals, carved images, or actual people are similarly used as scapegoats.

Scolopendra is a large, scaly ocean creature who plows through mighty waves with his bristling multitude of arms.

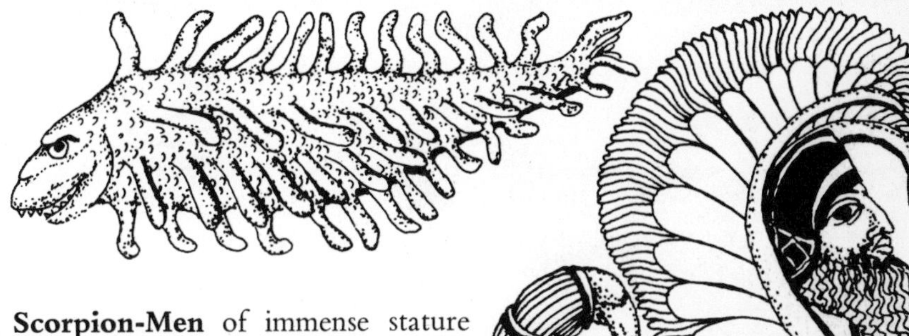

Scorpion-Men of immense stature and "dazzling brilliance" guard the gates to the mountain where Shamash, the **Sun** god, sleeps at night. They are partially scorpion, symbol of the soul that changes and is reborn, and partially angelic men. It was one of these cosmic creatures who showed the Babylonian hero, Gilgamesh, the long and difficult road to immortality.

Scylla was a pretty nymph whom **Circe,** the enchantress, transformed into a hideous, six-headed monster. Horrified at her ugliness, Scylla hides by underwater rocks in a narrow channel. Her barking heads, each with its triple row of teeth, gnash at passing ships, while her snaky tails slash the treacherous waters. Close by, across the straits, churns the deadly whirlpool, Charybdis.

Sea Horse is the fish-horse known as **Hippocampus.**

Sea Serpents are immense and monstrous snakes slithering their long, long lives away on deepest ocean bottoms. Sometimes, they rise up to devour a ship or two. More often they careen along in the distance, semisubmerged. The greatest of them all is the cosmic sea serpent, **Leviathan.**

Senex Maris, the Old Man of the Sea, is an ancient Greek sea god who herds his flock of smelly seals through the Mediterranean. Because he is a lover of truth and justice, his eyes are clear and have the power of seeing into the future. To question him, one must take firm hold of his slippery, slimy, and very smelly body and not let go. The Old Man will assume countless shapes, even becoming fire or water to try to escape; but if your hold is true, he will at last answer whatever of past or future you wish to know.

Shadows can only be cast by creatures that have a soul, therefore most magical beings do not own one.

Shaman or "curandero" is the powerful witch doctor of primitive tribes. He is a man so rigorously trained that, in his ecstasy of wisdom, he can understand the speech of birds, animals, plants, and stones. He uses this knowledge to guide his people through the destructive natural forces that surround them. He explains mysteries to them and cures illnesses of mind and body. Often during their rituals, shamen wear masks representing the animals whose protection they seek.

Shee, or Sidhe, are the stately **Tuatha De Danann** fairies of Ireland. In India, a Siddha is a free and perfect being, living between heaven and earth.

Shojo is the happy Japanese spirit of sake, or rice wine. His friendly little face is usually flushed with drink or excitement. It is said that he came to Japan from across the sea. He can often be seen romping and dancing along the shore—his red-gold hair spraying out about him and reaching right down to his toes. Somehow, however much he may drink, his ladle is always full of sake.

Sileni are very wise, but very drunken, old men. They ride around the Greek countryside on shaggy asses, although some people believe that they have the back legs of horses. They often accompany the goat-legged **Satyrs** in their reveling attendance on the wine god, Dionysus.

Simurgh, or Senmurv, is a fantastic Persian bird, similar to the **Phoenix.** Enlightened King of Birds, even his bright feathers have great magical and medicinal powers. He lives eternally in a distant and inaccessible mountain. There have been brave birds who, having undergone serious hardships to reach him, realize at last that the answers to the questions they wished to ask are already hidden deep in their own souls.

Sirens are misty, lovely bird-women who perch on high cliffs overlooking the sea. With their magical songs, they charm sailors to sleep; then, swooping down like birds of prey on the drifting ships, the musical Sirens tear the slumbering men limb from limb. Later, the Sirens were said to have **Mermaid** tails and to die if their songs go unheeded.

Si-Si-ootl is the magical, two-headed sea snake of the Canadian Kwakiutl Indians. It can change its size at will, and a small human spirit face peers from the center of its body. It is inauspicious to see the Si-Si-ootl, but a piece of its skin brings luck to the hunter.

Skinfaxi is the horse most loved by travelers because his shining mane spreads golden streaks of light across our skies. He is the Teutonic steed of Day, handsome grandson of Night, whose own wild, dark horse is called **Hrimfaxi.**

Sky Pinto of the Navaho Indians is a heavenly blue pony with white, cloudy spots. His mane and tail billow out behind him as wind-streaked clouds. His hooves beat like distant thunder as he gallops down from the sky to carry the souls of the dead braves far away to the happy hunting ground.

Sleipnir is the swift, eight-legged stallion of Odin, Lord of Teutonic Gods. He was born from the fire god, Loki, disguised as a mare, and the horse of a giant who built the walls of Heaven. Astride faithful Sleipnir, great Odin often traveled to and from the Land of Death. In many traditions, an eight-legged horse carries spirits to the other world, and, in India, a bier, always carried by four men, is called a horse with eight legs.

Snakes and serpents, in many cultures, represent wisdom and knowledge. Because knowledge misused or misunderstood is extremely dangerous and harmful, these legless creatures have come to be called the messengers of evil.

Sorcerer, from the Latin word "sors," or fate, is one who can divine the destiny of man through the use of secret arts. They are often semi-divine people, and, usually, the greatest are female. A sorceress is mistress of the mysteries ruled by the moon: mysteries of magic herbs and changing shapes. She can control the weather and make plants bloom out of season. **Circe** is among the most renowned of sorceresses.

Sphinx, in Greece, was a being half woman, half winged-lion. Perched slyly on a cliff top, she massacred all who were unable to answer her riddle: "What walks on four legs in the morning, two legs at midday, and three legs in the evening?" When Oedipus came by, he answered at once: "Man crawls as a baby on all fours, then walks upright, and in his old age leans on a cane." When she heard this, the Sphinx was so angry that she hurled herself to death on the jagged rocks below. The better-known Egyptian Sphinx has the head of a man, so the Greeks called him **Androsphinx.**

Spider Woman was a beautiful young American Indian. Powerful and wise, she led her people far up the West Coast of the United States to the edge of the icy North Pole. Then she became too proud and called on her people to use magic to melt the snows and cross over. But the gods saw her audacity and became very angry that she should try to change the face of the earth. So they cursed her to grow old and evil and never to die. Now she lives at the top of a tall rock. When a child is naughty, she creeps down to the canyon below and snatches up the little offender to her nest of sun-bleached bones at the top.

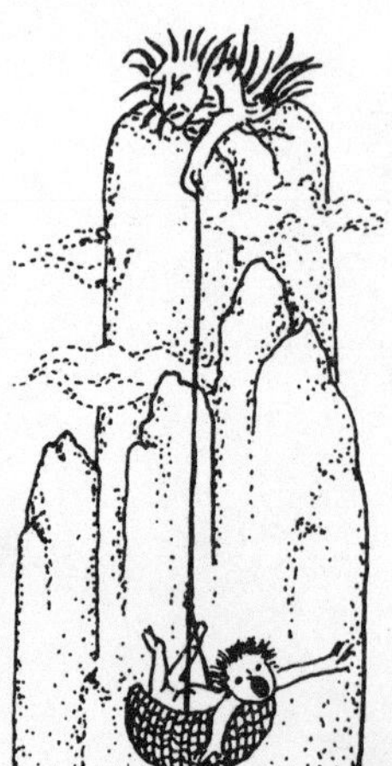

Sprites and Spirits are all the energy creatures that have neither shape nor substance until they enter the body of another being and become its spirit. They are usually gentle, as are the **Nymphs, Elves,** and flower sprites, but some are malignant: trees that grab at travelers or gnarled root spirits that trip them in the dark.

Stags of Cerynea are celestial deer sacred to the Greek **Moon** goddess, Artemis. Their antlers are pure gold, and their brassy hooves ring musically over the stony hills where they wander.

Stymphalides were man-eating, iron-clawed birds. Hercules, the Greek, frightened them away forever by banging loudly on cymbals.

Su, or Succarath, is a ferocious beast that lives in the cold, wild country at the tip of South America. Half tiger and half wolf, it has the head of a beautiful but malicious woman. Its tail looks like a large, flat, green palm leaf. If it is cornered by a hunter, the mother Su will kill her young rather than let them live in captivity.

Succubi are the female **Incubi.** They are demons who are both born from, and produce, bad dreams.

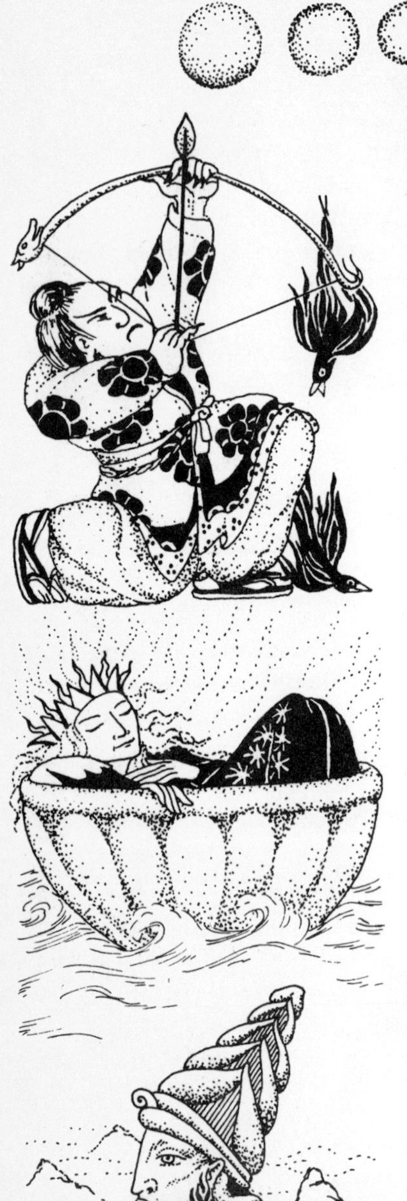

Sun, as giver of heat and light and, therefore, of life itself, has been a focus of worship in most cultures.

In China, it is said, there used to be ten suns who perched all day in a mulberry tree and took turns in lighting the earth. One day, all ten decided to rise into the sky together, and the incredible heat of so much fire began to destroy the earth. Immediately, the gods sent for **YI, THE DIVINE ARCHER,** to shoot down the extra suns, which feat he soon accomplished, the dead suns falling at his feet in the shape of ravens. Yi left only one sun—the one we see today—burning in the sky.

The early Greeks worshiped **HELIOS,** the beautiful young sun god who drives his four-horse chariot daily from east to west across the sky. At night, afloat in a golden cup, he sails back along the River Ocean to his starting place.

PHOEBUS-APOLLO, the brilliant, is a later Greek solar deity. Famed both as artist and healer, many followers came to his oracle at Delphi to ask their fate.

Another sun god famed for his soothsayers and diviners is the Babylonian, **SHAMASH.** Daily, he rises from the Mountain of the East, guarded by the gigantic **Scorpion Men.** He is an all-seeing god, wise and fearless, who banishes the dark shadows and establishes law and order in the world.

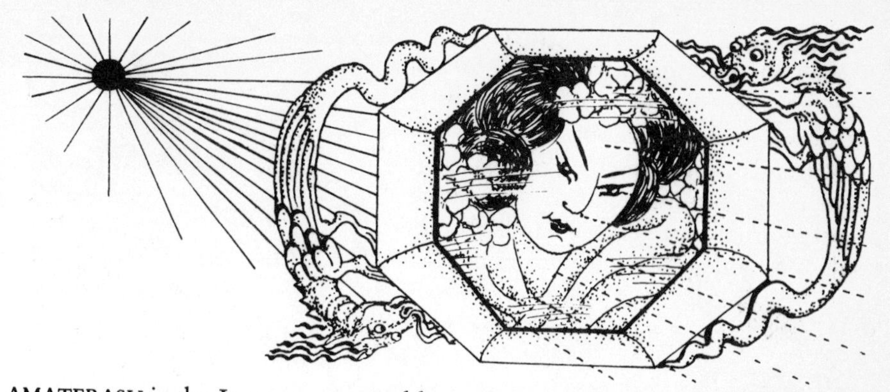

AMATERASU is the Japanese sun goddess. Once, terrified by her wild brother, the sea, she hid in a cave, leaving the world dark. There she stayed until, hearing a roar of laughter, she peeked out and saw the gods enjoying themselves as a goddess danced. The gods, having thus succeeded in luring Amaterasu from her cave, convinced her not to hide again by giving her an octagonal mirror which she may enter whenever she wishes to attend a ceremony.

The ancient Egyptian Sun gods were the falcon, **Ra,** and the scarab, **Khepri.**

SURYA is the magestic Indian Sun who regulates all things. He has three eyes and four arms, and his red skin was so dazzling that, until part of his light was shaved off, even his wife tired of looking at him. His chariot is drawn by seven horses or by a seven-headed mare, driven by a legless charioteer. Surya dispenses life and understanding. He also replenishes the moon with the divine Soma, elixir of inspiration, which nourishes alike gods, men, animals, and plants.

Swan Maidens are strange, lovely bird-women of Teutonic mythology. Often, they fly through the sky in the shape of swans, like a flock of white clouds on a clear day. At times, they remove their swan dresses, revealing their enchanting girlish forms as they swim and play in lonely mountain lakes, far from mortals with their curious eyes. If, while she is naked, a man should seize her plumy dress and hide it, the maiden is bound to obey his will. Whatever of the future he wishes to know, she must reveal to him and she must stay with him until he returns her feathers. It has happened, sometimes, that of her own accord, a Swan Maiden falls in love with a human. In that case, she may marry him if she wishes and accompany him at all times, either as a swan or as a woman, without losing her magic.

Sylphs are the **Elementals,** or spirit people, of the element Air, of which their bodies are entirely composed. They are fluid and graceful, tall and thin. It is almost impossible to glimpse one wafting by because of their rarefied nature.

Syrinx was the pretty Greek **Nymph** loved by **Pan,** the wild goat-god of Nature. To escape his amorous clutches, she fled in terror. As she reached the riverside, the gods, hearing her pitiful cries for help, transformed her into a flock of reeds by the water's edge. Pan, unabashed, cut down the reeds and formed of her lithe body the pipes through which he whispers his melancholy love songs.

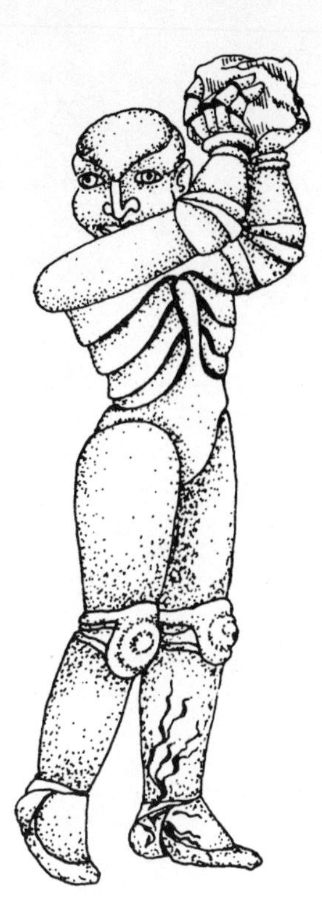

Talos was a giant bronze robot who guarded the little island of Crete. He was the last survivor of the ancient race of bronze men and would have lived forever had he not had one small vulnerable point: his life was contained in a small, blood-red vein in his ankle, stoppered up with a bronze nail. At last, the sorceress, Medea, pulled out the nail and the giant's life flowed away.

Tarasque of Tarascon was a beastly **Dragon** defeated by Saint Martha in the countryside of medieval France.

Taraxippos, the "horse scarer," is the ghost of a wicked Corinthian who used to feed his horses on human flesh. Finally, the ravenous horses devoured their own master. In revenge, his spirit became a ghoulish specter who commonly lurks on race tracks. Invisible to the jockeys, Taraxippos leaps out at the galloping horses, causing them to start and shy in terror.

Tengu is a winged old demon who lurks in Japanese mountains. Perched crowlike at the top of a pine with his sword and cudgel, he refreshes himself with a large feathered fan while waiting for a victim. As soon as a lonely traveler approaches, he springs down and cruelly attacks him. However, if properly propitiated, he can be bribed into teaching a warrior the fine art of swordsmanship, at which he is highly skilled.

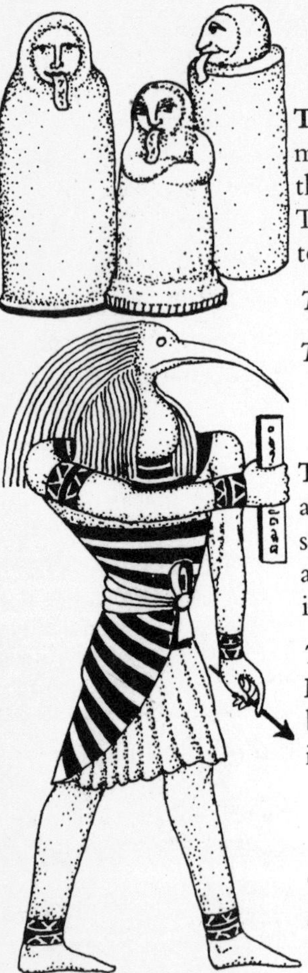

Teraphim are small figurines or mummified **Heads** mentioned in the Bible. Under their tongues is a thin piece of gold inscribed with magical words. They are often consulted as oracles by the family to whom they belong.

Terpsichore is the **Muse** of lyric poetry and dance.

Thalia is the ivy-wreathed **Muse** of comedy.

Thoth is the ibis-headed Egyptian god of learning and communication. He taught the people to observe the movement of stars, how to calculate with arithmetic, and how to express themselves in writing, painting, and music.

Thugs are the Indian version of the wild Greek **Maenads.** They are fanatical worshipers of the blood-loving goddess, Kali, who tramples the earth in her mad victory dances.

Tiamat was the terrible and bitter watery serpent of chaos in Babylonian mythology. From her sprang all the gods and also all the demons. Finally, the gods killed her. They then took half her body to make the heavens above and the waters below; with the other half, they made the earth.

Tigers in China are appointed to rule over the four Cardinal points: the fiery Red Tiger of summer rules the South; North belongs to the Black watery Tiger of winter; to the East lives the Blue spring Tiger of vegetation, while the West is governed by the White Tiger of autumn and metals. In the center of the world, where the ancient land of China stands, lives the fifth Tiger who commands and controls his four brothers; and his color is Yellow. These tigers guard the four corners of the world against all the fighting demons.

Tiki was the first ancestor of man in Polynesian mythology. Soon he got tired of being alone in the world, so he patted a mound of sand into the shape of a child. Three days later when he came back to the beach, the sand child had grown into a living woman. He called her Earth Maid, and she became his wife, the first woman. Now, Tikis are the kind and protective ancestor spirits of all Polynesians. These spirits inhabit small, carved figurines which the island people wear around their necks as talismans to bring good fortune and avert evil.

Titans, children of the Earth and Sky, were the ancient **Giant** gods of the Greeks. Their reign was called the Golden Age when the gods walked upon the earth and all things were peaceful and harmonious. But the Titans became tired and degenerate, and soon their own sons, the young Olympian Gods, led by thundering Zeus, overthrew them and cast them deep into the bowels of the earth. From this dark prison, their mighty rumblings still cry out for freedom.

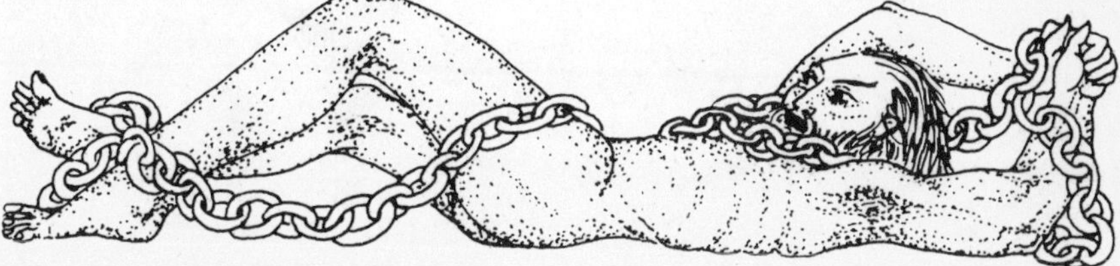

Toads in some traditions are called emissaries of the devil, but more often, they are considered beneficent water spirits. To own the jewel that sprouts on the toad's forehead is very lucky. It is a powerful charm against poison and will warn the possessor of approaching danger by changing color and sweating violently. The queen of the Gypsy fairies rarely appears any more, but when she does, she discreetly takes the form of a golden toad. And everyone, of course, knows that toads often turn out to be princes after all.

Tomtes and Tonttus are, respectively, the Swedish and Finnish versions of the **Brownie.** They are active, happy creatures whose laughter often rings through the farmhouse. Rather shy, they are seldom actually seen and they are small enough to sleep comfortably on a furry mitten or warm, woolly sock. If well fed and provided for, they return the hospitality by increasing the harvest and wealth of the farmer.

Tortoise is one of the great magical figures of China and Tibet. It is made of starlight, and wise men know the future by reading the cosmic messages written on its curved and mystical shell.

Tree Geese, or Barnacles, are a small variety of marsh goose that abound in Ireland. Unlike other birds, they are not hatched from eggs but rather ooze out of driftwood as a sort of resin. They remain attached to the log all the while their feathers are sprouting. Once fully grown, they let go of their woody mother and either fall, swimming, into the water, or fly away.

Triton is a huge Greek sea god, son of Poseidon and the nymph, **Amphitrite.** He is man to the waist, tapering into a long, scaly fish tail below. As time went by, he multiplied, until now there are hundreds of Tritons swimming the seas and oceans. They all love the adventure and excitement of tempestuous weather, so they carry graceful, curvy conch shells on which to whistle up winds that, sweeping from the sky, billow the stormy waves.

Troglodytes are a race of elephant-headed men encountered by a European adventurer on his travels through mysterious Africa. This imaginative explorer, who also reported **Crane Men** and various other strange tribes, died without leaving word as to whether these people lived—like the troglodytes of today—in underground caverns and dark passageways.

* **Trolls** are horrid, ignorant monsters of Scandinavia. They come in all sizes and look rather like the place in which they live: a Forest Troll resembles a deformed and bristly pine while a Cave Troll looks more like a lumpish clod. They may have any number of heads, fingers and toes, or none at all, but most of them do have tails. Always lurking in the shadows, Trolls will burst to smithereens if the sunlight touches them. Malicious, spiteful, and selfish, they should be studiously avoided.

Tuatha de Danann, or "People of the Goddess Danu," were an early race that invaded Ireland. Tall, noble, and generous, they were finally defeated by new invaders. They were driven back to the hills where they moved underground, living in earth mounds called "sidhe," or "shee." There, they lived in worlds where barriers of space and time did not exist. Soon the memory of this glamorous "lost" race was deified by the Irish people and they came to be considered as nature gods. In later times, seldom seen and even more shrouded in mystery, the Tuatha de Danann were called simply Shee, the **Fairies** of Ireland.

Typhon is a Greek monster whose hundred fiery snake tongues shriek and bellow with the voices of both men and beasts. Imprisoned by the gods under Mount Aetna, even today, one can feel him thrashing about underground and see his fiery spit well up from the volcano's ominous crater.

Undines are the water spirits, highest of the four kinds of **Elementals.** Generally feminine, they are very wise and may even acquire a soul by marrying a mortal man.

Unicorns were proud, fierce little creatures, symbolizing purity and truth. They looked like small horses, with the hooves of a deer and a lion's tail. They were so pure and so magical that, if their single, twirly horn were dipped into a sea of poison, the water would instantly become clean and drinkable. In spite of its diminutive size, the Unicorn was a ferocious and indomitable being with a terrifyingly loud, trumpeting voice. Only a virgin could approach this most mystical of all animals without fear. At the sight of her, it stopped its fearsome rampage and, becoming gentle as a fawn, laid its head sweetly in her lap. The Unicorn became extinct when it was elbowed out of Noah's Ark by the other passengers.

Uraeus is the terrible, sacred asp of Egypt. It coils its scaly body about the Pharaoh's crown, spreading its golden hood above his forehead. If an enemy dares come near, the Uraeus instinctively senses the danger and, spitting poisonous fire, instantly strikes him dead. It is often associated with **Ra,** the Egyptian Sun God, and can be seen encircling the sun disk above this god's falcon-shaped head.

Urania is the stately **Muse** of astronomy.

Urchins are small, mischievous fairies. The term has come to apply also to small, mischievous boys, especially the kind that run ragged and laughing through the back streets and alleyways.

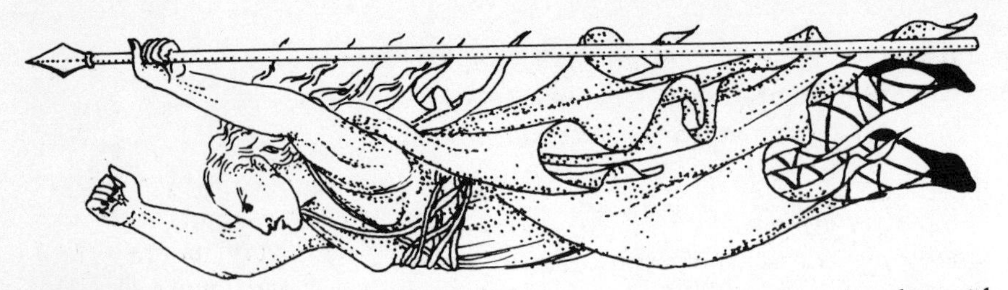

Valkyries are semidivine, Scandinavian warrior maidens. Fiercely, they ride their airy horses into battle or fly above the warriors, choosing among them which are to win and which to lose, which will live and which of them must die. When the fighting is over, these stately, beautiful women lead the noblest among the slain to the great hall, Valhalla, where heroes feast eternally.

Vampires are the bloodsucking bat-people of Slavic folklore. Many, including the famous Count Dracula, live in the mountainous country of Transylvania. A Vampire is an unblessed corpse inhabited by an evil spirit. At night, the reanimated corpse assumes the shape of a bat and, flying through open windows, sucks the blood of sleeping humans, who then become Vampires themselves.

Vanir are the oldest race of Teutonic deities. They are fertility gods who, commanding both wind and rain, regulate weather, crops, and marriage. Best-loved among the Vanir is Freya, exquisite goddess of love and beauty, and her handsome brother Frey, Lord of the Nature **Elves,** who rides the golden boar, **Gullinbursti.**

Vegetable Lamb of Tartary is the mossy sheep otherwise called the **Barometz.**

Vodyanye are wicked, treacherous, Slavic water creatures. They may assume any shape they choose: ugly or beautiful, fish, plant, or human. They never die but do grow older at the waning moon and younger as it waxes every month. They live in fresh water and especially like to gather near water mills and make loud splashing noises in hopes that a human being or two will fall into the water out of fright. Whenever the Vodyanye do manage to drown someone, or, if a person is thrown to them as a sacrifice by the miller—which is very pleasant—they take the human to serve them as slaves in their magical underwater palace of crystal.

Volva, in Teutonic mythology, was a wise woman who, long after she was dead, could be induced by magic to come back to life just long enough to prophesy. Then, having answered the questions put to her, she was allowed to die again.

Vritra was the Indian demon of drought and other weather unfavorable to crops. By practicing great austerities, self-sacrifices, and meditations, he became equal even to the gods in power. Able now to perform miracles and create illusions, he upset the balance of nature with his evil forces. The only one left powerful enough to fight him was Shiva, the fertility god, who had built up his powers with yoga and meditation. Finally, Shiva managed to defeat Vritra and bring rain back to the earth, so that crops could grow again and nature take her course.

Warlock is one of the officials in a **Witch** ceremony, although male witches are often so called.

Weird or Wyrd are alternate spellings of Urd, the chief **Norn,** queen of fate and death.

Werewolf is a man who willingly or not has sudden fits of becoming a wolf. These fits usually occur about the time of the full moon, when his body actually becomes that of a wolf. In animal form, he races wildly across rocky mountains, howling at the moon and attacking every living thing in order to drink its blood. In his daily life, he usually looks quite normal except that his hands may be slightly gnarled and his nails a little too long and sharp. The werewolf disease is called Lycanthropy.

Whirlpoole is a huge, whirling, swirling, huffing, water-spouting variety of whale. It is also called the puffing Physeter, from the Greek word meaning "blower."

Will-o'-the-Wisp is a mischievous sprite who, dressed in a wisp of blue boggy flame, darts about the marshes at night. It is best not to annoy him, for once he gets hold of someone, he doesn't let go.

Witches are men and women who worship and pay homage to the goat god of nature and fertility, a descendant of the lively Greek god, **Pan.** Because, in the West, the devil is thought of as goatlike and because many of the witch ceremonies are cruel and orgiastic, they have been accused of worshiping the devil. Many Christian rites have been incorporated into their otherwise pagan faith. They assemble regularly in groups or "covens" of thirteen members, the leader of which is almost always a woman. They also have festivals called Sabbat which are attended by many covens. Their main concern is the acquisition of power through the study of herbs and the mysterious ways of nature.

Wizards are men who, through their wisdom and learning, become more than human. They often wear tall, conical caps like inverted megaphones through which they receive cosmic messages. They know the movement of stars and have found the paths of dragons. Knowing the laws of the earth, they are almost all-powerful and cannot be harmed. Merlin, greatest of all known wizards, was said to be the son of a nun and an **Incubus.**

Wraith is the ghostlike image of a person that is soon to die. Sometimes near a moonlit graveyard a procession of ghosts drifts by and flitting among them is the shadow of a man still alive. The man himself may be far away and unaware that his image is out walking with the dead. Before the week is out, that man will die. A person may also meet his own wraith just before his time to die has come.

Xanthus and Balius, sired by the West Wind and the **Harpy,** "Shining Foot," were the immortal horses of the Greek, Achilles. The goddess, Hera, gave Xanthus the power of human speech so that he might warn his master of his death. But the **Furies,** who dislike unnatural things, immediately took away this power in case the horse should be tempted to reveal to men the secrets of the gods.

Xnoumis, or Chnoubis, is the Agathodemon, Good Genius of the Gnostic religion. A beneficent sun god, he is shown as a huge serpent with the head of a lion. He is crowned with twelve rays representing the zodiac, the band of constellations through which the sun travels each year. He is also a god of healing and a renewer of life—as symbolized by the serpent that sloughs off its old skin.

Xochipilli, the Aztec "Prince of Flowers," is usually represented with a skull in place of a head. He and his twin sister, **Xochiquetzal,** the "Flower Bird" are gods of love, joy, beauty, and youth. They live high in the mountains surrounded by musicians, dancers, and all the bright-eyed flowers of spring. As green and fruitful gods in a dry land, they are among the best-loved and most joyfully celebrated of all the ancient Mexican deities.

Yakshas are grotesque but kindly little Indian demons, children of Night. They guard the rich treasures of the world—stored high in the Himalaya Mountains. Their king, Kubera, is a small, deformed dwarf with three legs and pallid skin. Although hideously ugly, he is very friendly and usually more than a bit drunk. At one time in his life Kubera did penances and practiced yoga, for which the gods rewarded him by allowing him to live forever as guardian of the northern part of the world. When he rides out in his chariot, jewels spray from it, scattering across the earth.

Yale is a large, black-dappled deer with a boar's snout. Its graceful horns are so loosely attached to its head that they can be moved at will. When fighting, the Yale swings one horn forward to attack with while keeping the other one back for "just in case."

Yamato-No-Oraichi was the eight-forked storm dragon of Japan. A rampaging pest, it was finally overcome by the god-hero, Susano-O-no-Mikoto. When he cut into the dragon's tail, he found there a magical sword called "sword of the gathering clouds in heaven."

Yemanja is the beautiful Brazilian ocean goddess. Every year the people go down to the shore and throw her offerings of flowers, beads, and trinkets. If she is pleased she brings fish to the fishermen and good luck to all. Sometimes, when a man has swum too far out to sea, she appears—radiant amid the waves—holding out her arms to him. As he embraces her ecstatically, they both disappear beneath the water, and the man, happy now forever, never returns.

Yeti, the Abominable Snowmen, are huge hairy men living high in the Himalaya Mountains. Seldom have more than their gigantic human footprints been seen in the snow. But lonely hunters tell of being fiercely attacked by Yeti. A few holy men claim to own hairy Yeti scalps, which they consider sacred. In the Americas, Big Foot and Sasquatch, similar creatures, have been reported.

Yllerion are a pair of fiery birds with sharp pointed wings. After living sixty years, they hatch two eggs then plunge to their death in the sea. All the birds of the air escort them on their last flight and then return to raise the two little chicks until they are old enough to live alone.

Zaratan is a wondrously huge sea monster who, slumbering lazily, floats on the waters like an island. It can drift in this semisleeping state for years, until plants and even trees sprout up along its back. Terrible tales have been told of unwary sailors who, passing by and mistaking the monster for an island, drop anchor and go ashore on its broad back. When they build a fire to cook their evening victuals, the heat of the flames penetrates down through the thick, scaly skin and the beast leaps in agony from its peaceful dreaming. With a heart-freezing bellow, it dives to the deepest ocean, dragging with it all the unlucky men, ship, anchor, cookpot, and all.

Zarathustra's Ass is the mystical servant of the God of Light. It is a pure-white ass with three legs ending in enormous hooves, six triumphant eyes, nine mouths, and one hollow golden horn with which it punishes the wicked. Like the **Unicorn,** it purifies poisoned waters.

Ziz is the gigantic bird who with the ox, **Behemoth,** and the fish, **Leviathan,** represent all living creatures.

Zombie is a new corpse whose soul has been stolen by the Voodoo Man. The zombie must work for its master until such time as it can eat salty food. This breaks the spell and allows the zombie to return to its grave.

The End

Selected Bibliography

Andersen, Hans Christian. *The Complete Andersen.* Translated by Jean Hersholt. New York, Heritage Press, 1952.

Bible: King James Version. New York: Humphrey Milford, n.d.

Borges, Jorge Luis. *The Book of Imaginary Beings.* New York: E.P. Dutton &Co. 1969.

Bratton, Fred Gladstone. *Myths and Legends of the Ancient Near East.* New York: Thomas Y. Crowell Co., 1970.

Briggs, Katharine M. *The Anatomy of Puck.* London: Routledge & Kegan Paul, 1959.

Bulfinch, Thomas. *Bulfinch's Mythology.* New York: Random House, Modern Library Edition, 1934.

Byrne, M. St. C., ed. *Elizabethan Zoo.* London: F. Etchells & H. Macdonald, 1926.

Christie, Anthony. *Chinese Mythology.* London: Paul Hamlyn, 1968.

Clebert, Jean-Paul. *Les Tziganes.* Paris: Arthaud, 1961.

Cohen, John. *Human Robots in Myth and Science.* London: George Allen & Unwin Ltd., 1966.

Davidson, H.R. Ellis. *Scandinavian Mythology.* London: Paul Hamlyn, 1969.

Dorson, Richard M. *Folk Legends of Japan.* Vermont and Tokyo: Charles E. Tuttle Co., 1962.

Dutt, Romesh C. *Ramayana/Mahabharata.* New York: E.P. Dutton, Everyman's Library, n.d.

Evans, Bergen. *Dictionary of Mythology.* Lincoln, Nebraska: Centennial Press, 1970.

Frazer, Sir James G. *The Golden Bough.* 1 vol. abridged ed. New York: Macmillan Co., 1940.

Gardner, Edward L. *Fairies: A Book of Real Fairies.* London: Theosophical Publishing House, 1966.

Ginsberg, Rabbi Louis. *Legends of the Jews.* 8 vols. Philadelphia: The Jewish Publication Society of America, 1911-1938.

Gould, Charles. *Mythical Monsters.* London: W.H. Allen & Co., 1886.

Graves, Robert. *The White Goddess.* New York: Stratford Press, 1948.

The Greek Myths. Baltimore: Penguin Books, 1955.

Grimm, Jacob and Wilhelm. *The Fairy Tales of the Brothers Grimm.* Translated by Mrs. Edgar Lucas. London: Constable, 1909

Ions, Veronica. *Indian Mythology.* London: Paul Hamlyn, 1967.

Koran. Translated by J.M. Rodwell. London: J.M. Dent & Sons Ltd., 1957.

Lang, Andrew, *The Crimson Fairy Book.* London: Longmans, Green & Co., 1903.

The Blue Fairy Book. London: Longmans, Green & Co., 1897.

The Brown Fairy Book. London: Longmans, Green & Co., 1904.

The Green Fairy Book. London: Longmans, Green & Co., 1895.

(New) Larousse Encyclopedia of Mythology. 2d ed., rev. London: Paul Hamlyn, Prometheus Press, 1968.

Leach, Maria, ed. *Standard Dictionary of Folklore, Mythology, and Legend.* New York: Funk & Wagnalls, 1949.

Lull, Ramon. *The Book of Beasts.* Translated by E. Allison Peers. London: Burns, Oates & Washbourne, Ltd., 1927.

Lum, Peter. *Fabulous Beasts.* New York: Pantheon Books, 1951.

Mackenzie, Donald A. *Teutonic Myth and Legend.* New York: W. Wise & Co., 1934.

MacManus, Dearmuid A. *The Middle Kingdom: The Faerie World of Ireland.* London: Max Parrish, 1959.

Mandeville, Sir John de. *Travels.* Cambridge, England: Cambridge University Press, 1950.

Mardrus, Dr. J.C. *The Thousand Nights and One Night.* Translated by Powys Mathers. London: Routledge & Kegan Paul Ltd., 1964.

McHargue, Georgess. *The Impossible People.* New York: Holt, Rinehart and Winston, 1972.

The Beasts of Never. New York: Bobbs-Merrill Co., 1968.

Ovid. *Metamorphoses.* Translated by John Dryden. New York: Heritage Press, 1961.

Ozaki, Yei Theodora. *The Japanese Fairy Book.* New York: Dover Publications, 1967.

Pliny. *Pliny's Natural History.* Translated by Philemon Holland. Edited by J. Newsome. Oxford: Clarendon Press, 1964.

Polo, Marco. *The Travels of Marco Polo.* New York: Grosset & Dunlap, n.d.

Silverberg, Robert. *The Realm of Prester John.* New York: Doubleday & Co., 1972.

Tripp, Edward. *Crowell's Handbook of Classical Mythology.* New York: Thomas Y. Crowell, Co., 1970.

Waley, Arthur, trans. *Monkey.* New York: Grove Press, 1958.

Waters, Frank. *Book of the Hopi.* New York: Ballantine Books, 1969.

White, T.H., trans. *The Bestiary, a Book of Beasts.* New York: G.P. Putnam's Sons, 1954.

About the Author

Paulita Sedgwick, artist, actress, and scholar, although born in the United States, spent the first year of her life in Haiti. It was there, she believes, as she was rocked to sleep by the sound of voodoo drums, that her interest in magical things unfolded. It has not left her since. Paulita Sedgwick has traveled the world over, living in North and South America, Europe, Africa, and Asia. Throughout, as she pursued her various careers, she studied the subjects of greatest interest to her—religion and mythology. She now lives in New York, where she appears in off-Broadway productions and continues her other work and studies. She is the illustrator of *The Pluperfect of Love* by Dorothy Crayder and *Ancient Egypt from A to Z* by Barbara Pradal Price.

About the Book

The book was set by film composition in Griffo and illustrations were executed in pen and ink.